WOMEN AND POVERTY

First published in 1989 by
Attic Press, in conjunction with The Combat Poverty Agency
44 East Essex Street,
Dublin 2.

British Library Cataloguing in Publication Data
Daly, Mary
    Women and poverty
    1. Poverty - Sociological perspectives
    I. Title
    305.5'69

ISBN 0-946211-62-0

Cover Design: Paula Nolan
Typesetting: Phototype-Set Ltd.
Printing: The Guernsey Press Co. Ltd.

The views expressed in this book are those of the author and do not necessarily represent the views of The Combat Poverty Agency.

MARY DALY is a sociologist now working as head of research with the Combat Poverty Agency. Her publications include *The Hidden Workers* (EEA 1985), *Local Planning* (IPA 1987) with Laraine Joyce and *Moneylending and Low Income Families* (Combat Poverty Agency 1988) with Jim Walsh.

CONTENTS

ACKNOWLEDGEMENTS

This book would not have been possible without the help of many people. I thank the following especially: John Blackwell, Heather Brett, Noreen Byrne, Anna May Harkin, Liz Hayes, Nuala Kelly, Mary Lyons, Frank Mills, Angela Mulligan, Jo Murphy Lawless, Pat O'Hara, Cathleen O'Neill, Joy Rudd and Marie Walsh. Many groups and organisations also helped, among which I owe a special debt to local women's projects. The assistance given by Tim Callan of the Economic and Social Research Institute and Eoin O'Broin and Seamus Bradley of the Department of Social Welfare is also gratefully acknowledged. I would also like to thank my publishers, Attic Press. I owe special thanks to my colleagues at the Combat Poverty Agency. Hugh Frazer gave me the encouragement and the space to write the book. Brid McGrath unfailingly and generously tracked down material for me. Jim Walsh's perceptive comments and very generous help throughout were invaluable. The help given by Margaret Barry, Helen Burke, Ann Cronin, John Hynes, Noreen Kearney, Ellen Kennedy and June Meehan is also gratefully acknowledged.

My greatest debt is to the many women who shared their experiences so openly with me. Their trust will not be forgotten.

A special thanks to Heather Brett, Rita Ann Higgins (and her publisher Jessie Lendennie), Carmel McCarthy, Cathleen O'Neill and Moira Stowe for permission to reproduce their poems.

For Joan, my mother

INTRODUCTION

Women are one-third of the world's formal labor force and do four-fifths of all informal work, but receive only ten percent of the world's income and own less than one percent of the world's property.(1)

The reality of poverty in Ireland is now beyond doubt. Compelling evidence exists, and not for the first time, showing that poverty is a fact of life for many in this country. About a third of the Irish population are living in poverty, depending on how it is measured.(2) 34% of Irish people were living below a poverty line equivalent to £48 a week for a single person or £81.60 for a married couple in 1987. On the basis of these figures, the amount of poverty in Ireland grew by between 2% and 4% since 1980. With the cutbacks in public services, very limited growth in jobs and the inadequacy of social welfare payments, poverty will continue to increase in Ireland unless action is taken.

Widespread poverty exists amidst plenty in this country today: Ireland is currently the 27th richest country in the world (out of 160 nations). Some people in Ireland are very wealthy with top salaries now exceeding £150,000 a year, and it is possible for some people to make the same again by sitting on the boards of a number of companies. In January 1989 *Irish Business* magazine identified forty-five of the most wealthy individuals in Ireland. Between them they had wealth in excess of £1 billion. None were women. Compare this kind of wealth with the fact that nearly 70% of people in Ireland say that they cannot afford a week's holiday away from home.(3) Work is not the only way to amass large amounts of money. The property boom in Dublin, for instance, made fortunes for some people, while at the same time placing the price of a home of their own beyond the reach of many, particularly the young. This is the other side of poverty.

Women and Poverty

In spite of growing awareness of the existence of poverty, very little information exists about poverty among Irish women. We can estimate the numbers of women living below a poverty line but we have little comprehensive and accessible information on what life is like for women living on low incomes. Until now there has not been a specific investigation of women's poverty in Ireland. At best, women have been an addendum to research focusing mainly on men or, more often, information is not analysed by sex. The huge gaps in information about poverty among Irish women precipitated this book. Without adequate information and analysis, new and effective policies to address women's poverty are unlikely to be developed.

Changes now taking place in Ireland put women at greater risk of poverty. They include population changes - such as increasing marital breakdown, more children being reared by one parent families and growing numbers of elderly women. Economic changes are also key, having led to very high unemployment and a growing number of low paid jobs. There is also an increased reliance on women's unpaid work, as public spending on services, especially health services, is cut back. In many countries there is an emerging phenomenon known as the feminisation of poverty where women are forming an increasing proportion of the world's poor and are more visible in their poverty than ever before. In the United States of America, it is estimated that two out of every three poor adults are women; in Britain 40% of all households headed by a woman are poor.(4) Many other countries have also experienced a growth in female poverty - usually because of increasing numbers of one-parent families and continued low wages for women at a time when their economic responsibilities have never been higher.

Perceptions of Poverty

The true extent of poverty is still not widely accepted in this country. Yet the facts are available to show that poor people exist side by side with a majority who have a fairly adequate, if not a comfortable, standard of living and a minority who are very well off. One hears many excuses: there is no 'real' poverty in Ireland today compared with the 1930s and 1940s;

no one needs to be poor now with social welfare; people are poor through some fault or failing of their own. Each of these statements is rooted in particular beliefs. The first in the belief that there is only a single type of poverty, one that involves absolute destitution and deprivation. The second belief is that the social welfare system eliminates poverty; the third that people have equal access to resources and opportunities and therefore everybody has the possibility of getting on. Each of these is false.

Poverty is not only about basic physical survival but must be measured and understood in the context of the standards of living and lifestyles of the population as a whole. So, being poor today is very different from the poverty of earlier times - people do not have to be destitute to be poor now. The second argument - that social welfare eliminates poverty - is also untrue. Ending poverty is not even a stated aim of social welfare; its main purpose is to provide a subsistence income for those who cannot keep themselves, that is, to sustain people at a basic level. With regard to the argument that it is the poor's own fault, resources and opportunities are not distributed equally: some people have more than others and easier access to education to begin with and therefore are better placed to prosper and advance themselves.

What is Poverty?
Even though it is a widely used term, poverty is a difficult concept to define and understand. Yet it is important to arrive at an acceptable definition of poverty, not just for its own sake but also because doing so helps us to identify the measures necessary to eliminate it.

Poverty is mainly associated in the public mind with money and material well-being. One of the most enduring questions about poverty is whether it should be treated as absolute or relative. Treating poverty as absolute is to equate it with physical survival, ie enough money to provide sufficient food, clothing and shelter just to survive. Talking with people who are themselves poor shows how this view of poverty fails to take into account people's other needs (social, emotional, political and cultural) and that there is much more to life than having enough food and clothing to survive. Yet the notion

7

that poverty is absolute and that there is a magical cut-off line is remarkably persistent.

Relative definitions, which put poverty in the context of average standards of living, are now much more popular.(5) In this view, poverty is a matter of degree; needs are socially determined and people are poor if they cannot obtain the resources to participate in their local area or society. Thus, the poor are excluded from a standard of living similar to that of the majority of the population. A broad definition of poverty underlies this book.

Understanding Women's Poverty

Although, of course, poverty is not confined to women, the focus of this book is primarily on women's poverty. The extent of poverty among women is looked at, along with women's experiences of what it is like to live on low incomes. Developing an understanding of women's poverty requires analysis, as well as description, however. So, women's experience in the home and family, with work, social welfare, public services such as health, education and so on, are considered for their effects on women's chances of escaping from or ending up in poverty. A central task is to examine the extent to which state structures and economic forces create or reinforce divisions among women, and between women and men.

What we are referring to here is where and how women fit into existing structures and particularly their access to resources and opportunities. The most important resources for getting on in Ireland, and elsewhere, are education, a well-paid job, good health and capital and other assets that can make money. To understand why some women are poor, we must consider women's access to resources and opportunities, accepting from the beginning that resources are not shared equally, that is, that inequality exists.

What determines access to resources? The explanatory framework for this book rests on two key factors: class and gender. People are grouped on the basis of their socio-economic position, especially their occupations. Those sharing a similar position form a class. Classes are marked by the differences or inequalities between them as much as by the similarities within them. Access to, control over and ownership of resources are limited to people with certain characteristics, especially those in the upper classes. This makes it difficult, in some cases impossible, to move from the class into which one was born.

But class is not the only determinant of life chances. Men across classes generally fare better than women in the same class. So, the concept of gender is also central. Gender is the process whereby differences between the sexes are built into structures, so that men generally are more powerful than women and men's interests dominate. Using a framework that involves both class and gender means that we will not treat women who are poor in isolation from other women, or from men. In concrete terms, this means that we cannot explain women's poverty without reference to some women's power over others and also to poverty generally as a product of class structures. This is a structural view of poverty: access and control over resources determines who is poor and who is not.

Using a class and gender framework has difficulties, however. To begin with, it is an enormous task to fully explore and explain the interaction between the two forces. There is only limited existing work to call on; usually poverty has been examined in Ireland in the context of class. Not only this, class analysis has focused on men. Women, then, have been largely excluded from the analysis. This has given rise to a second set of difficulties: shortage of information, and limitations in existing information. Because relatively little has been written about women on low incomes in Ireland, a central aim of the book is to provide new information on women in this situation. Some information gaps simply could not be filled, however. So, among other things, we are unable to compare the situation of women on both sides of the border, a regrettable loss since north/south relations have had a significant influence on the position of women and the women's movement as well as all other aspects of life on this island.

There are other gaps in our information. This is especially true in the case of women living in rural areas and also women who are emigrating now or those who have emigrated in the past. We have no idea why they are leaving or what happens to them subsequently. So, these and other topics are not covered in the detail they deserve. Lack of information on Irish women also forces us to rely in places on evidence from other countries.

The Measurement of Poverty and Women

Placing the focus on women means that we must look critically at how existing research has treated women. Research can conceal as well as reveal. Most poverty research has shortcomings in how it has measured poverty among women. Conventional research on poverty has usually assumed that income is distributed equally within the home. So the research has based its measures of poverty on the income of collective or aggregate units such as families and households. This ignores both the possibility that income is unequally shared and women's lack of control over the family's income. Women, therefore, and perhaps children also, are likely to be undercounted in poverty figures that are based on household or family income. Research based on household or family income accepts that there are no poor people in households or families with incomes above the poverty line and that all members of families are equally poor or rich. Such assumptions are unjustifiable in the absence of evidence to prove that they are correct.

Where possible throughout this book, women living on low incomes speak for themselves, sometimes through their writings and poems. This kind of information is as important, and in some cases more important, as statistical information. Women's own experience of poverty is the main focus of interest throughout this book.

The Framework for the Book

The main dimensions of women's poverty provide the book's structure. The book consists of three parts: the first descriptive; the second explanatory; the third suggested changes.

Chapter 1 presents and examines the most up to date evidence available on poverty in Ireland. Women's poverty is the main focus and the characteristics of groups of very poor women are examined in detail.

Chapter 2 puts flesh on these statistics: it describes, sometimes in women's own words, what it is like to live one's life in very poor conditions. We get a feeling for women's everyday lives, their hopes, fears and expectations.

Chapter 3 takes work as the focus and looks at how women fare with regard to paid work and unpaid work and how they have been affected by recent developments in the labour market.

Social welfare's treatment of women is examined in Chapter 4, particularly for its effect on women's long-term chances of remaining in or escaping from poverty.

In Chapter 5 the focus is on women's access to public services, mainly education, housing and legal services.

Chapter 6 looks at the relationship between women's health and poverty.

Chapter 7 examines some local actions that have been taken to improve women's situation, especially attempts by women to organise themselves in their local areas. The purpose is to evaluate the potential of educational activities among women at local level for bringing about change.

Chapter 8 looks to the future and identifies the possibilities and priorities for action to address women's poverty.

NO VACANCIES

Heather Brett

There is only one chair by the fire,
my chair; the children sprawl on the sofa
or the floor, soles upwards and there is
a lack of family portraits.
There is no man in this scene.

This morning I opened the windows wide
to let your scent go, but all day I could
smell you, feel your skin on mine like
a pressure, like the imprint of fingers
after the grasp is removed.
Tonight I sit in my chair, in my house
The children draw and chatter about the
coming communion. There is an audible silence
when they are quiet and I wonder if it is me
who wedges open these small spaces - and for what?

I did not give you my chair last night.
There are boundaries everywhere that you
cannot cross, and I am quick to mention them
too quick, perhaps, to put you in your place
too quick, also, to assume mine.

Alone I look fondly on the things we
have here, the bits and pieces that I have
accumulated and collectively call mine.
The walls are missing nothing, the house
is furnished, we call it home.

All the rooms are taken and each bed is spoken for
any cracks have long since been papered over or
filled in. We have no space left, no empty drawers
or anywhere where another might make himself at home:
There are no candles burning in the window.

1

THE NATURE AND EXTENT OF POVERTY AMONG WOMEN

Women are the poorest of all. Women are responsible for family finances but they have none of the power that goes with possession. Having it in their hands never made money their own.(6)

The Measurement of Poverty in Ireland

Poverty is always being 'rediscovered' in Ireland, as elsewhere. The first of the recent 'rediscoveries' here was at a catholic church-organised conference on poverty in Kilkenny in 1971, at which it was estimated that at least 24% of the population were living in poverty. Within a short time, poverty had become a political issue at national as well as European level: the first European programme to combat poverty, which provided funding for local projects and research on poverty for a five year period, was started in 1975. Ireland lagged behind other countries in 'rediscovering' poverty: in Britain and the United States of America poverty came to the fore as an issue in the early and mid 1960s. The 'rediscovery' of poverty in these countries involved three stages: counting the numbers of people in poverty; public discussion and lobbying about poverty; acknowledgement by the state of poverty's existence.(7) It is worth noting that 'rediscovering' poverty does not necessarily involve state action to deal with it.

Poverty was 'rediscovered' here yet again in the early 1980s as further research was published.(8) During late 1988 and early 1989, public and media interest in poverty was rekindled, precipitated by, among other things, the the launch of research by the Economic and Social Research Institute (ESRI).(9) Counting how many people are poor has proved very difficult. Both technical and political problems exist. The most common approach is a narrow monetary one: taking a poverty line or income cut-off point and counting as poor all those with incomes below the line. Even this is not straightforward however. To begin with, there is the problem of where to draw the line. Most research in Ireland has used the basic level of social welfare payments to derive a poverty line, usually 20% to 40% above them.(10) This is unacceptable, however, because social welfare rates are not set according to how much money people require to meet their needs, but by a complex political budgeting process where the government works out how much it is willing to pay people on social welfare. A second source of problems with poverty lines is that, because they rely only on income to measure poverty, they ignore other important resources, such as education, property and other assets, and they almost totally exclude lifestyle differences.

The ESRI research, however, avoided using social welfare rates, instead choosing poverty lines in relation to average incomes. Information was obtained from over 8,000 people all over Ireland, in 3,300 households, about their income from all sources, their living standards and how much money they thought they would need to stay out of poverty.

How Many People Are Poor in Ireland Today?
The ESRI research is convincing about the wide extent of poverty in Ireland in 1987. Taking three different income cut-off points (worked out in relation to income levels across Irish society), between 13% and 34% of people in this country are living in poverty. At the lowest poverty line of £32 a week for an adult (and its equivalent for other family sizes)(11), 13% of people are poor. If a cut-off point of £40 a week for one adult is taken, 23% of people are poor. Finally, setting £48 a week for an individual adult as the poverty line, 34% of people are on incomes less than that. The research itself did not choose a poverty line, recognising that there is no such thing as an objective poverty line. The trap of poverty lines should be avoided because they are so misleading. The concept of an adequate basic income is a better approach. The ESRI research showed that a majority of Irish people now believe that between £55 and £65 a week for a single person is necessary to avoid poverty. So, by Irish society's own standards, *a minimum of 1 in 3 people are living on inadequate incomes*. According to the ESRI research the

14

situation is getting worse: the numbers of people in poverty increased at a faster pace in the 1980s than in the 1970s.

Who Are the Poor?

Poverty is highly selective, it only affects very specific groups of people. According to the ESRI's findings, today's poor are mainly the unemployed, large families, some farming households and those who are ill or disabled. Unemployment has a major impact on poverty: a third of all households living on incomes of less than the equivalent of £40 a week for one person are headed by an unemployed person. Rural poverty, especially that associated with small farms, is also widespread. Family size is closely related to poverty; the more children a family has the more likely it is to be poor. Over 6 out of every 10 households below the lowest poverty line (ie on incomes of less than the equivalent of £32 a week for an individual) contain children. In general, children in Ireland have a greater risk of poverty than adults.

Poverty Among Women

The ESRI researchers had little to say in the first report about either the scale or the nature of women's poverty. Analyses of the data by sex carried out specially for this book by the ESRI show that 274,000 adult women (compared with 244,000 adult men) live in households below a poverty line of £48 a week for an adult in 1987. This means that slightly over 30% of both women and men are living on incomes below this level. Women in rural areas have a higher risk of poverty than women in urban areas. Age also affects women's risk of poverty: those between the ages of 35 and 64 years are at a higher risk than women in any other age group. Separated women are also a very high risk group.

The ESRI data show only part of the picture of poverty among Irish women, however. Because this study is based on *households*, and tax units to a lesser extent, it provides little information on women who do not head households or those who do not pay income tax. The figure of 274,000, then, refers to the number of women who live in households below the poverty line, and excludes women who are poor in other households. The study also adopted a limited approach to poverty, seeing it mainly in terms of income and relying on the poverty line concept. Consequently, the figures should be taken as estimates only of the number of women in poverty in Ireland. We need to examine information from other sources if we are to develop a more comprehensive picture.

The security of income source is a very important influence on poverty, along with the actual amount of income. Women's incomes are much less secure than those of men. Even though the number of women in employment has grown over the last twenty years, less than a third of Irish women earn an independent income through paid work, compared with 60% of men. Women therefore are more vulnerable than men to poverty. The following groups of women appear to be most at risk:

* women rearing children on their own
* elderly women
* 'minority' women, especially travellers and women who find themselves homeless
* women in low paying jobs
* some women working full-time in the home.

Women As Lone Parents
One adult households with children are the most likely of all types of household to be poor, in Ireland as elsewhere. The majority of lone parents world-wide are women and the majority of these women are poor.(12)

In the 1986 *Census*, there were 81,087 households consisting solely of a lone parent with children. The vast majority of these (82%) were headed by women. There are more mothers rearing children on their own than this, however. A special analysis of the 1986 *Census* data for this book identified 85,693 mothers who were not living with a man.(13) The majority (64%) of these were widowed, 17% were married, 11% were separated and 7% were single. Between them these women had over 160,000 children, ie an average of two children each. Only slightly more than one in five were working outside the home. Separated and single mothers were the most likely to be in employment (see Table 1). Most of these working mothers were in fairly low-level jobs, mainly service and industrial work. Only 16% were in professional occupations.

16

Table 1:
Occupational Grouping of Employed Lone Mothers

	Widows %	Separated %	Married %	Single %	Total %
Production work	35	14	14	24	26
Transport	2	3	3	4	2
Clerical	10	24	19	23	16
Commerce	16	13	15	12	15
Service workers	22	25	16	23	22
Professional	13	17	30	10	16
Others	2	3	4	5	3
Total	10,028	5,254	2,159	2,239	19,680
% of total	18	35	22	36	23

(Source: *Census of Population, 1986*)

It is difficult to know the income source of the majority of these women lone parents. At the end of 1987, about 30,000 women rearing children on their own were in the social welfare system. If we add to these the 20,000 identified by the *Census* as working outside the home, it still leaves over 35,000 women lone parents whose source of income is unknown. Those who are depending on private maintenance arrangements with their husbands, partners or other family members may be experiencing hardship. Research on 1,127 applications for maintenance orders through the courts over the last ten years highlights the inadequacy of many private maintenance arrangements.(14) In 60% of these cases, the woman was awarded less than £32 a week and only 9% of maintenance orders were fully paid up. Over half of all the orders investigated were in arrears for six months or more. The procedures available through the courts for maintenance had been exhausted in most cases.

Families headed by a woman on her own are becoming increasingly reliant on social welfare. The number of women claiming 'deserted wife's' payments, for instance, doubled over the last ten years. Some mothers on their own also have difficulty in getting maintenance from the state. The conditions attaching to the 'women's schemes' (ie 'deserted wife', 'unmarried mother', widow, 'single women', prisoner's wife) can be difficult to satisfy. Peter Ward's research found a 57% success rate among a sample of 266 applications for 'deserted wife's' payments over the last seventeen years, for instance. While valued for its security, welfare can be degrading for women rearing children on their own. Applying the cohabitation rule for instance - where welfare officials seek to establish whether a woman claimant is having a relationship with a man - can be deeply invasive of a woman's privacy.

The number of one-parent families is growing in Ireland, as elsewhere. By 1986 the number of one-parent families had grown to over 97,000, making up 10% of all private households in Ireland. Trends in Ireland may soon mirror those in Britain where one-parent families were the fastest growing group in poverty during the 1970s.(15) One-parent families now make up nearly half of all the families living in poverty in Britain. Such trends are seemingly universal: between one-quarter and one-third of all families worldwide are supported by women and these families have been found to be leading candidates for poverty and hardship.(16) One of the main reasons why one-parent families have both a high risk of being poor and of staying poor is because they are denied access to the most effective route out of poverty: full-time employment for both parents.(17)

Elderly Women

In Ireland in 1986, there were 384,355 people aged 65 years and over, representing 11% of the population. The numbers of elderly are growing all the time so that there is a general ageing of the population - as people are living longer we have more old and very old people. Women dominate the over 65s in greater numbers as one moves up the age range: 56% of all those over the age of 65 are women, but women are two-thirds of all those who reach 80 years of age. Although the ESRI research suggested that poverty among the elderly had declined between 1980 and 1987, the general consensus of research is that more women than men end their lives in poverty.

There are a number of reasons for this. First, women live longer; since old age is closely associated with poverty, women predominate among the aging poor. Secondly, women are poorer before they reach old age - throughout their lives they have had less access than men to all kinds of resources but especially employment (and therefore occupational social welfare benefits, including a contributory pension). Women, then, are less likely than men to have savings and assets with which they can supplement their income when they are older. Thirdly, elderly women are more vulnerable to poverty, isolation and loneliness because the majority of them are either widowed or single, whereas the majority of elderly men are married. Finally, and related to the previous point, women are more likely to live alone - for every one man over 65 years of age living alone there are two women. Living alone is closely linked to poverty among the elderly - a recent study found that 73% of the elderly living alone fell below a minimum income standard.(18)

The situation here is similar to that elsewhere. In Britain, for instance, a hierarchy of financial security exists among the elderly. Couples are the most secure, then men on their own and finally lone women.(19)

Women in 'Minorities'

Two groups of women have an especially high risk of poverty in Ireland: women from the traveller community and women who are homeless. Many in these groups are excluded from conventional poverty research: they are unlikely to appear in the recent ESRI research, for instance, because it is based on a sample of the Register of Electors and they are rarely registered.

Traveller women are at a very high risk of poverty, not only because they are members of a community that is itself very vulnerable to poverty but also because of their lower status within that community. At the time of the last *Census* of travellers in 1986, 7,863 women travellers were enumerated (there were 7,883 men).(20) Life is very harsh for traveller women: on average the *Census* showed that women tend to marry very young, raise ten children, have a high risk of losing some of their children at birth or in early childhood, and will themselves die at a younger age than women in the settled community. Life is lived in very poor conditions - nearly half of all traveller families still live in caravans, a quarter on the side of the road. Think what this means for a woman trying to care for her large family without basic amenities like piped water, electricity, toilet facilities. And on top of this there is isolation, rejection and prejudice from many people in the settled community.

Women who find themselves homeless are among the poorest of all. No exact figures are available on the number of women who are homeless but the number is known to be increasing. Frequently, women do not appear in the homeless statistics because they receive help from their families or friends. One study estimated that homeless women could have numbered over 9,000 in Dublin alone in early 1984, commenting:

> *One of the most important things to emerge from this study is the extent to which the homelessness of women in Dublin is hidden. Women tend to go to friends or relatives much more readily than to hostels and because of this their homelessness is not visible to the public eye. (21)*

Women often become homeless trying to escape violence and other forms of abuse within their homes. Between June 1987 and June 1988, one shelter in Dublin - Brú Chaoimhín - had 259 residents, two-thirds of whom were women who had been battered.(22) The facilities for homeless women are quite inadequate in Ireland - although the voluntary organisation, Focus Point, which works with homeless people has developed interesting settlement strategies.

Women on Low Pay
Work is generally regarded as an escape from poverty. This is not always the case, especially for women. Up to 15% of those who are currently poor are in the workforce. Research carried out recently, based on information from 1979, estimated that almost half of all women workers then were low paid, ie on wages of £65 a week or less.(23) In numbers this was equivalent to 44,000 women workers. Unfortunately, the information to update this research is not available.

While low paid female employees were in many different types of job, they were most likely to be working in industry and in wholesale and retail distribution. The 'cheap' jobs are familiar: some factory work, shop and supermarket work, waitressing and other jobs in catering, cleaning, hairdressing, and so on. Women are a majority in all these types of job; a situation that has not been changed significantly by the existence of the Employment Equality Agency and the equality legislation. The inescapable fact is that women's labour is cheaper than that of men.

Women are lower paid than men also because they form a greater proportion of the part-time workforce. Over 70% of part-time workers are women, most of them married. Part-time work is less well-paid than full-time work. Low pay is not the only disadvantage of these kinds of jobs. Because most part-time jobs are outside the control of the authorities, their conditions of work are usually far from satisfactory. For instance, part-time workers rarely qualify for protection under the employment legislation, which means, among other things, that they can be dismissed without a stated reason and treated more or less as the employer likes. More women will be relying on these kinds of jobs in the future given the likely permanence of high rates of unemployment and the fact that the government is placing increased reliance on the service sector as the source of future job creation. In the long-term, this may not be to the advantage of women.

Another measure of women's disadvantage in employment is to compare their wages with those of men. Again, the results are not encouraging. Women in industry now earn only about 60% of the average male weekly wage. This proportion has never been higher than 68%, even in the 1970s after the equal pay legislation was first introduced. Again, it comes back to the fact that women's labour is cheaper than men's and that, when they do find jobs, many women end up in work that is lower paid and bears a close similarity to the jobs they do within the home.

Women in the Home
Women working in the home are usually involved in caring for others, either for children, the sick, the elderly or their husbands, and sometimes for all these. This is the single largest group of women in Ireland: nearly 700,000 women of working age in this country are based full time in the home.

Yet their economic and other circumstances are almost totally hidden from view. Being unwaged, they are dependent on their partners for their income. It is not known how many women in this situation get sufficient income because no research in Ireland has looked at how income is shared within the home. The ESRI research, for instance, cannot be relied on to identify the extent or degree of poverty among this very large sector of women, except those who are defined as heads of households. So, there are no reliable figures on poverty among women engaged in 'home duties'.

Other evidence indicates that some women in this situation may be poor. In a recent study, 14% of all families studied had serious money problems because men were not transferring sufficient income to their wives.(24) Research has repeatedly shown that separated and divorced women perceive the poverty of lone parenthood to be an improvement on their economic circumstances in marriage. (25) Eileen Evason, for instance, found that while 70% of the lone mothers she studied in northern Ireland were living in poverty, nearly a half of the divorced and separated women felt that they had the same or better living standards when on their own. Other feminist research has challenged many of the conventional assumptions about women and men and the sharing of income within the family.(26) It has shown that resources are not shared equally within families, and that by managing scarce resources women help to either prevent greater poverty in the family or to protect men and children from its worst effects.

One group of women whose circumstances should be looked at closely is those caring for the elderly at home. 66,000 elderly people are estimated to be cared for in their homes in Ireland, more than three and a half times the number in institutional care.(27) Over 70% of the carers are women. The experience of caring is quite different for women and men. Women carers usually live in the same household as the elderly person, which means that they will be providing care for longer periods, and they get less support than that usually received by male carers.

So, a minimum of over a quarter of a million Irish women are living in financial poverty today. These women may be in different living situations but there are three characteristics that they share: *motherhood, dependency status,* and *under-paid or unpaid work.*

OFF THE WALL

Cathleen O'Neill

The scream started again to-day
A slow silent scream of frustrated anger.
    Today I wailed at the wall of officialdom

Smug, smiling, filing-cabinet face,
    Closed to my unspoken entreaty
Social justice is my right
Don't dole it out like charity!

Robbed of Independence, dignity in danger
I stood, dead-locked, mind-locked.
Helpless in his sightless one-dimension world
    I walked away
My mind screamed a long sad caoin for the us
    And
Damned their 'Social Welfare'.

First published in *Notions*. Dublin: Klear/Borderline, 1987.

2

WOMEN'S EXPERIENCE OF POVERTY

Sometimes I blame my husband - he has been out of work over three years now... But then sometimes I blame myself, I think it's all my fault, I must be doing something wrong to be in this mess. But I'm trying so hard really, that's all I'm doing is trying so hard.

So said Sarah, who is 34 years of age with eight children, aged from 15 down to 1 year. She lives with her husband and children in a large suburb on the west side of Dublin. The total family income from unemployment assistance is £157 a week.

Statistics are technical things which have little meaning in day-to-day terms. It is easy to become caught up in poverty lines or income cut-off points, but what are they after all only measures developed by researchers for their own purposes. You cannot see a poverty line and it conveys no sense of what life is like for a woman in Sarah's situation. Also, single income cut-off points hide the severity of poverty and blur differences between people who live well below it and those just on or above a poverty line. Women themselves are not often heard in research, especially if they are poor. Personal experiences have been afforded little space in quantitative research on poverty, or on other topics.

Here we listen to women talking about their own experience of living in poverty. The information comes mainly from conversations with many women living in different degrees of poverty around the country. Individual and group conversations were held in which a number of themes dominated: the hard work and drudgery of life in poverty, the feelings of inferiority and powerlessness, the anxiety and worry, not for themselves so much as for their children, the loneliness and isolation. The results of other research are also used where available.

Dimensions of Poverty

Although not always experienced in the same way, poverty usually involves a struggle to survive - eking out a limited income on a daily basis, dreading an expected expense, and terrified of an unexpected one. Life with little money can be very drab - homes need money for their upkeep and repair, new or, more likely, second-hand clothes have to be bought and almost every activity involves some spending, even if sometimes very small amounts. Most of us have little realisation of just how much an extra 20p spent or saved can mean to someone living on a very low income. Bus fares can be luxuries for people who are poor. It is not unusual for people in the suburbs of Dublin to make only one trip to the city centre a year.

Day to day, most people can manage - they may do so by borrowing - but they manage. What is hardest is the longer-term - facing the next electricity bill, the children's return to school for the coming term or year, a crisis in the family. Some women hate to look ahead:

> I *can't bear to think of the future. I won't let myself think even as far as next Christmas. It's too up-setting - it is as if I have no future. Nor do my children. Will they have jobs?*

The hard work that poverty entails comes across in practically all conversations with women who are poor. Making meagre ends meet uses immense labour and energy. Trailing on foot around often distant supermarkets and shops for the best bargain - sometimes saving no more than a few pence - queueing, constantly on the lookout for goods reduced in price, keeping the children entertained so that they will not notice their hunger so much, going from agency to agency to provide evidence of one's need for welfare purposes.... the list is endless. In certain areas it can be even more difficult because of distance and high prices charged by shops which have no competitors.

Of course, these activities absorb more than labour: they are also very time consuming. Time is never considered as a valuable resource, except when it is paid time. Women's time is generally perceived as being without value because so much of it is unpaid. Managing an inadequate income takes an immense amount of time and skill. Saving money is hard work, it often involves substituting time for money: walking instead of driving or taking the bus, washing clothes by hand in order to save electricity, and so on. Very poor households cannot afford labour saving devices, such as washing machines or microwave ovens. Time for herself is often the greatest luxury for a woman; if she is poor it can be difficult to get.

> I think women really need a break from the house. But it's different for a woman, she just can't get up and go the way her husband does. Just take this morning. My husband wanted a message in town so he just got up and headed off. Before I could come here I had to wash the breakfast things, clean out the fireplace, do the hoovering. Then I had to walk to the shops to get the messages for to-night's dinner. My daughter will be back at lunch time so I had to leave something for her lunch. It's like an expedition for us women to get out.

Poverty is demanding of another kind of energy as well: emotional energy. References to its emotional toll dominate women's conversations about their poverty.(28) Guilt, worry and fear are common. Guilt in relation to their children is especially widely experienced by women who are poor. Conversations come back again and again to their children. References to family obligations and family roles - as mothers, wives, daughters - are constant: women locate their own experience of poverty within a family context. Their role as mothers is predominant and notions of being a 'good mother' are held up as criteria for their failure. Most keenly felt are the inadequacies in the children's lives: poor diet, lack of warm clothes, being unable to afford healthy leisure activities for them, not having their own bed. Women feel responsible because they have to say no to their children all the time - they seem to internalise the blame for their situation.

Worry is another constant companion. Women who are poor have many worries: the next bill and the one after, a forthcoming visit to and from the community welfare officer, a birth in the family. Mothers worry about the escalating costs of children as they grow older. The fact that teenagers usually eat a good deal more than adults is never taken into account in social welfare payments. Apart from food, teenagers have other needs: fashionable clothes, discos, haircuts, sporting activities, and so on. Women also worry about what will happen when the children reach the age of 16 and are no longer eligible for social welfare payments if they are not in school. Will they be forced to become homeless to get a welfare payment of their own?

Money: Control and Management
A person's standard of living depends not only on the amount of money coming into a household but also on how resources are shared within families or households. The comforting notion that resources are shared equally among family members has always been taken for granted, without any concrete proof. Yet research in Britain has shown that nothing, whether it be work, money, time, help from relatives or food, is shared equally among family members.(29) Take money in particular: not only is there a distinction between its control and management but this distinction is gender-based: usually men *control* and women *manage* the money. As controllers, men make the key decisions about allocation and spending priorities. Women, on the other hand, as the managers, have the job of giving effect to the decisions taken by the man and providing for the family on a day-to-day basis on the money transferred to them, regardless of the amount. Being the controllers, either singly or jointly with their partners, men have greater power over, and usually first call on, the money. So, men may unquestioningly retain some social welfare money for their personal, usually leisure, use, even in families which are finding it very difficult to make ends meet. Women, in contrast, usually regard their portion of the income as being collective or family income, as 'housekeeping' money, sometimes even with money they have earned themselves.

The task of managing the money subtly transfers to the woman the responsibility for its adequacy or inadequacy - it almost becomes her fault when she cannot manage on the

27

money she gets. Women blame themselves for not being able to provide for the family's needs and they are often blamed by others.

> *Initially I took all the responsibility for all the bills, the children, household affairs. For example, when the ESB came to cut off the electricity, he (husband) refused to deal with them. Instead he came to me and said 'the ESB want to cut you off'. Recently, I went on 'split payments' as he was not giving me the social welfare money. I'm looking now for a separation... he has lived off me for long enough.*

The manager role also has other implications for a woman: she will bear the burden of borrowing - repaying money-lenders, for instance, is largely a woman's problem. Women also carry on much of the family's business with the state - they negotiate with state services, even though their applications are usually processed in the name of their husbands. Women usually hold out the family begging bowl: approaching the Society of St Vincent de Paul for charity; having their houses inspected by Community Welfare Officers to validate their request for help; asking for free school books from their children's teachers. As one woman said: *you learn to be a good asker.*

Contrary to popular opinion, women on low incomes not only budget but do so with great care and ingenuity. Recent research found that over 90% of a sample of very poor families budgeted very strictly.(30) Usually, money is first set aside for 'fixed bills' such as rent, fuel, debt repayments. Food is then bought from what is left over. Any money to spare after this is quickly absorbed by other necessities. Money is so tight in poor families that clothes and footwear are not normally budgeted for out of the weekly income - these are paid for by child benefit, if possible. Budgeting is often a matter of deciding which bills must be paid and which can be postponed until the following week. Of course, this is a short-term solution with adverse consequences: constant fears of a knock at the door, worry about having the electricity cut off, fear that the coal man will not supply coal the next time.

Poor money management and budgeting problems are often held as causing poverty, so much so that the state has given significant funding to the Society of St Vincent de Paul to teach the poor how to manage their money. And yet research by the British government has shown that the *poor buy more efficiently than the rich*: they get 33% more energy and protein per penny and a full 100% more of Vitamins A and D as well as other nutrients.(31) There is no evidence to show that this is not the case in Ireland as well.

Family Budgets

Rose, one child, on deserted wife's benefit		Joan and Tom, five teenage children, living on unemployment assistance	
Rent	£3.80	Rent	£9.10
Food	£20.00	Food	£49.97
Soap, washing powder, etc	£2.00	Soap, other toiletries	£6.09
Life assurance	£2.40	Assurance	£4.00
Electricity	£3.00	Electricity	£9.58
Fuel (coal)	£8.50	Fuel	£7.59
Television - rental	£3.80	Television - rental/	
cable link/	£1.40	licence	£6.20
licence	£1.20	cable	£1.20
Nursery	£5.00	Clothing/footwear	£7.00
Medical expenses	£2.00	Pocket money	£3.00
Bus fares	£3.00	Tobacco	£13.00
		Transport	£3.00
		Charities	.50
Total	£56.10	Total	£120.23
Total Income *	**£57.80**	**Total Income***	**£107.90**
Surplus for other expenses	*£1.70*	*Deficit*	*£12.33*

* Excludes child benefit and a £5 fuel allowance which is paid for 26 weeks of the year. When these figures are updated to take account of the changes introduced by the Budgets of 1988 and 1989, Rose's weekly payment would now be £66.80 while that of Joan and Tom would be £127.00, if their circumstances remained unchanged.

These are examples of how two families spent their money in early 1988.(32) Of course, this is only a snapshot of just one week out of fifty-two and gives little idea of the complex budgeting that frequently goes on in low income households and the financial pressures that arise at different points in time. They are useful, though, in providing a sense of the priorities and standard of living among poor families.

Not surprisingly, shortages and deficits are common. In the case of Joan and Tom, the deficit is over a tenth of their weekly income - it is made up by short-term loans from members of their family. In Rose's case, just £1.70 is left over each week to cover shoes and clothes, entertainment, special occasions, among other things. Among the most notable features of these two cases are how little Rose spends on food: just £20 a week for herself and a young child; and Joan's £13 a week on tobacco. She regards cigarettes as essential to her survival. Cigarettes are the lesser of two evils: if she did not smoke she would probably be on tranquillisers (which, of course, she would get 'free' from the state).

Survival Strategies
Women survive by using different strategies. *One strategy is reducing spending, mainly by cutting down on food and fuel.* Spending on food is not a fixed cost among poor households but varies according to the money available. Often food is the only area where savings can be made. The man and the children are put first: they get the best and biggest share of the food. For instance, when savings have to be made, the woman may not take any meat herself ensuring that others get some, or she may skip food at midday when the rest of the family are out. Lone mothers are particularly likely to cut back on their own food; it is more tempting for them to do so because they do not have another adult for whom to prepare a meal. Research shows that, following a separation from their partners, lone mothers used their greater control over their money to cut down their eating.(33) But the lone mothers in that study would not swap their situation to go back to their husbands: they might have had more money, but they also had far less control over it.

Cutting down on food in this way affects women's nutrient intake and in the long term their health. Research shows that in a poor Dublin suburb women eat less healthily than men or children.(34) Women's low iron, fibre and vitamin C intake, because they eat little meat and nutritious foods, is particularly worrying. In addition, they consume a lot of table sugar, mainly in cups of tea. The fact that children do not share their mothers' nutritional disadvantage shows that women sacrifice their own food intake.

Cutting down on fuel is another way of saving. There are a number of creative, but hard, strategies for this. One can, for instance, put the children to bed early, sitting on in the cold until one's own early bed-time. Another way of saving on food and fuel is to try and keep the children in bed until lunch-time at the weekends - this can save one meal in the day. Alternatively, extra layers of clothes can be worn.

Borrowing is a second survival strategy, usually it is money that is borrowed rather than goods. Weekly 'floats' - small amounts of money paid back almost immediately - are very common. Neighbours and family members help make up weekly shortages in income:

> *I couldn't live without my float. I get my money from my husband on dole day - Thursday. I do my big shopping that day at the supermarket. That's the day we have the best meal, usually with meat. From then on my main shopping is buying bread and milk at the local shop. By Monday or Tuesday I'm out of money. Then I borrow maybe £10 from my sister - she can give it to me because she gets her money on a Tuesday. I pay back what I owe her on Thursday so she can keep going.*

Borrowing is more extensive than this, however. Credit is a constant necessity for poor people and debt a constant reality. To live on social welfare long term means having little or no money put by, either in savings or for emergencies. This means that an unexpected expense, even a small one, can play havoc with the family's complicated financial balance. So the family, usually the woman, may be forced to borrow for quite small and routine expenses. For example, up to two-thirds of all loans taken out from moneylenders may be for routine expenses, such as electricity and other fuel bills, basic household goods and food (most of the other third are for 'family' occasions like Holy Communion, Confirmation, a wedding, birth or a death).(35) People who are poor have very limited access to formal sources of credit which means that they are forced to use expensive, informal credit, such as moneylenders. It is a vicious circle.

A third survival strategy is where a woman does paid work. The available work options are limited. Full-time work is often not only difficult for women on low incomes to obtain but it may be impossible because of family obligations. With so few state-funded childcare facilities, usually it is not worth a woman's time to work if she has to pay to have her children minded privately. Part-time work is often a more realistic option. However, the rewards are limited: part-time work is usually low skilled and low paid; cleaning work can still pay as little as £2 an hour for instance. Women are less inclined to take up paid work nowadays since the family's social welfare money will be cut if they earn more than £50 gross a week - an outcome of the implementation of the EC equality directive on social welfare in 1986.

The Social Costs of Poverty

People who are poor are defined as belonging to some category or other: *unmarried mother, unemployed, traveller, homeless*. These and other labels are stereotypes carrying certain expectations in the public mind: when you are poor you are not supposed to to go out for a drink, own a car or TV, smoke or dress your children well. Poor people constantly encounter these and other prejudices. They are often said to be poor through their own fault, therefore they are perceived as lazy, indigent, lacking in moral fibre and ambition. Lone women who are poor often carry the added stigma of being thought morally lax: they have children who are being reared outside marriage; their children are badly dressed, and so on. Lone women especially feel that other women regard them suspiciously. This makes them feel socially unacceptable as women on their own. In traveller culture, lone women parents have a lower status than mothers who are part of a couple.(36)

A good deal of stigma still attaches to being poor, especially in rural areas. Recently, there has been much public talk about social welfare fraud. Terms like sponger and scrounger are often used to describe all social welfare claimants. Yet in reality fraud is limited to a maximum of 4% of the 1.3m social welfare beneficiaries.(37) But name calling like *sponger* and *scrounger* adds to the burden that social welfare claimants carry.

Because of social stigma, people attempt to hide their poverty. Keeping up appearances takes many forms: a shut front door even on the hottest summer's day, never inviting callers in, ensuring that the children do not bring a friend home around meal times, borrowing clothes for occasions, excuses or claims of disinterest as a way of refusing invitations. A woman can take pride in hiding her poverty:

> *Would you have guessed how poor I am? I dressed up specially for you today. But these are not my own clothes. The skirt and shoes are my sister's, and the jacket belongs to a neighbour. We swap clothes all the time, even though mine are so bad that nobody wants them.*

Such borrowing may have to be returned, however, and many women fear the day when they cannot meet a request for help from a friend or relative. Clothes and other goods are also passed on from one person to another when no longer needed, 'pass-alongs' as they are called.

Conversations with women show that poverty is multidimensional. In their own words, poverty means:

* policing the kitchen at night so that the kids don't snack
* being tired of managing
* fear of children growing up accepting that this is what life is and not trying to get anything better from it
* having no choice about things
* having no money for clothes and living from the 'black bag' system of used clothes
* taking tranquillisers in order to be able to cope.(38)

So, we need a very broad view of poverty, especially when considering measures to eliminate it. In particular, we need to look at resources and where women fit into economic and social structures. Work, social welfare, public services and health are among the most important factors to be considered.

TO THE SISTERS IN THE WORKFORCE

Moira Stowe

Don't knock the woman
Who works in the house,
She's not a trail blazer
Or a meek little mouse.
Don't mock her or slate her
For not making a stand
But reach out and touch her
And please understand
She's doing her thing.
Right?

On the other hand

Women at home
Please prick up
Your ears,
There are women out there
Who are crying salt tears
For help in their struggle
To win equal rights
Just listen, don't knock them
They don't need a fight
With their sisters.

First published in *Notions*. Dublin: Klear/Borderline, 1987.

THE RELATIONSHIP BETWEEN WOMEN'S WORK AND POVERTY

> *... the contradiction between waged labour and domestic labour has not necessarily been resolved to women's benefit. In most cases where women go out to work, there is still housework to be done, and in most cases it is still left to women.(39)*

All women work and always have done. Yet most of their work is unpaid which makes them financially dependent - mainly on men or the state. The right to an independent income secured through paid work was one of the founding principles of the women's liberation movement. Feminists wanted women to be free to work outside the home or, in some cases, to be paid for their labour within it. A job is the single most effective escape route from poverty - it is through employment that most people get an adequate income as well as access to other resources.

There are two main ways in which work is connected with women's poverty:

* the majority of women are without an earned income of their own since they are involved full time in home work which is unpaid work
* when women are employed they usually earn less money than men, they work in lower level jobs and they may experience discrimination because they are women.

WOMEN WORKING FOR NO PAY

Most Irish women work for no pay - 53% of all women over the age of 15 are working full time in the home (see Table 2). Nearly 700,000 women, then, spend long hours caring for their families, and quite often for an elderly or ill relative as well, for no pay. The remaining women are either in the labour force (32%), in education (10%), retired or ill or disabled. Paid work is, therefore, secondary for Irish women.

Contrast women's situation with that of men - over 70% of whom are in the labour force (see Table 2). For every individual employed woman there are more than two men earning an income of their own. Only in their early twenties are women's and men's employment situations similar. After this, they diverge: women mainly to marry and/or to have children and remain within the home; men to continue in the labour force, either employed or seeking work, until retirement. Women's employment pattern is changing, slowly. More Irish women are working outside the home than ever before: the numbers grew by over 40% between 1971 and 1987. Most of this increase is due to greater participation by married women in paid work - growing by nearly 500% over the last fifteen years. Yet, in percentage terms, the proportion of women working outside the home is practically the same as it was at the foundation of the state: 32%. Today, about one in every five married women are in the labour force.

Table 2:
Women's and Men's Principal Economic Status in 1987

	Women 000s	%	Men 000s	%
In employment	352.5	(28)	735.1	(59)
Unemployed/seeking work	55.2	(4)	176.3	(14)
Home duties	669.8	(53)	5.5	(0)
Students	130.6	(10)	132.3	(11)
Retired	44.6	(3)	149.1	(12)
Ill/disabled	19.6	(2)	47.7	(4)
Others	7.9		4.8	
TOTAL	1,280.2	(100)	1,250.8	(100)

(Source: *Labour Force Survey*, 1987, Table 7.)

Women based full time in the home do far more than domestic work. In the farming community for instance, women make an enormous contribution: one of the main farming organisations recently produced evidence to show that a woman married to a farmer puts in between 50 and 60 hours a week on the family farm.(40) Add to this the secretarial and administrative back-up that women provide for most family-run businesses, including farms. Research into entrepreneurship, for instance, proves that most new businesses rely very heavily on the unpaid support and assistance of women.(41) We should remember also the contribution women make to the local community, providing, among other things, a network of care for the elderly, the ill and disabled and children that saves the state a lot of money.

Agriculture more than any other sector shows the grey area between household work and market or paid work: women's contribution to the farm household is impossible to distinguish from the farm as a productive unit. So, there is undercounting of women's contribution to agriculture. National accounts statistics undervalue and give no economic value to a lot of women's labour. When domestic labour is costed, the result is astonishing. A very conservative estimate, based only on a 37 and a half hour week, in 1984, valued work in the home at nearly £3 billion (equivalent to about 18% of Gross Domestic Product).(42) *It is not that women do not work, rather that much of their work is unpaid, which is a very different thing*.

Consequences for Women

While not forgetting that many women choose or prefer to be based full time in the home, such high levels of non-employment have serious consequences for women, not all of whom may be aware of them. For a start, it means that most women do not have an independent income of their own: two-thirds of Irish women are financially dependent either on men or on the state. While not all of these are in the same situation, the incomes of a substantial minority are low and may also be insecure. Because of the way poverty has been measured, we do not know precisely how many men fail to hand over sufficient money in the home. Not earning increases women's risk of poverty in another way as well - two-earner households have a much better chance of avoiding poverty than households with only one income. Consider what a woman gives up by remaining in the home. To begin with, just consider the earnings she foregoes - British women are estimated to lose a minimum of £135,000 in earnings over their lifetime because of their family responsibilities.(43) This would actually be a conservative estimate for Irish women who are far more likely to permanently give up full-time employment to care for their families. An Irish woman working in industry at 1987 pay levels who leaves her job at the age of 27 and never returns to paid work will forego at least £200,000 in earnings over her lifetime. And this takes no account of the extra time (above the 40 hours working week norm) a woman will put into her caring role. It takes mothers about 50 hours a week just to feed, wash, change nappies and perform other services for pre-school children.(44)

Spending a considerable part of her life in the home significantly disadvantages a woman in other ways as well in our society: it does not confer any qualifications, it does not count as work experience and the skills developed are not perceived as employable skills. Yet they are used all the time in jobs, eg managing money and other resources. Women working long-term in the home are also excluded from social welfare benefits in their own right (ie payments made on social insurance contributions) like contributory pensions or disability benefit. One of the worst catastrophes that can befall a family is when the mother becomes ill - social insurance does not cover this and there is no compensation for families who have to employ somebody to carry out the mother's work.

As well as these drawbacks, joblessness leads to exclusion - from rewards such as status, from opportunities for self-fulfilment and self-development, from social contacts and networks. Powerlessness and joblessness often go hand in hand because it is through their jobs that most people get a chance to influence decisions. Obviously, it is not only women who are jobless, but more women than men are systematically excluded from the labour market, from access to an independent income and from being considered as workers, even though they work very hard. Even the terms used to describe and classify work - a job, employment - refer only to paid work, which automatically excludes the majority of women's labour.

One way of reducing women's poverty would be for women to be paid fully for their work. Women should have the choice of working outside the home and being paid an adequate wage, or of receiving an independent income while working full time in the home. Employment by itself is not the solution - for many women it is too poorly paid and they

38

prefer to be full time mothers. An adequate, independent income is what women need.

Among the reasons why more married women are now employed is because they are having fewer children and also because of the removal of obstacles like the marriage bar in the public service. However, Ireland still lags significantly behind other countries: an average of 40% of EC women were in the labour force in 1986, compared with our 32%.

Why Don't More Irish Women Work Outside the Home?

As we have seen, being married still makes a big difference to Irish women's employment situation, while it makes no difference to men's work patterns. However, when we ask women themselves we find that it is not so much marriage as childcare which determines whether they are in a job or not. *74% of married women (and 44% of women generally) say that they are not in a job because of their children or more precisely because of their childcare responsibilities.*(45) Only 2% of men give this reason: education, learning new skills and widening their opportunities, along with unemployment, are the main factors that take men out of the labour force. Some women leave the workforce to rear their children and then find it difficult to get back in. Working in the home is not always a choice for women - as many as a third of married women say that they regret not having a job. Economic factors are not the only concern: 'housework is basically dull and boring' and 'being at home with the children all day can very often be boring for a woman' were views shared by 68% and 76% of a sample of Dublin women and men in 1986.(46) Housework is likely to be even more boring, and certainly more arduous, for women who live in poor conditions: old and shabby rooms are much harder to keep clean, as are cheap clothes for children and adults. Inexpensive goods break down more often and wear out faster than costly items.

The barriers that prevent women or make it difficult for them to take up a job are crucial to any discussion of women's poverty. While they apply to women in other circumstances as well, women on low incomes have fewer resources to enable them to overcome these barriers and at the same time a greater need of additional income. Three main barriers make it difficult for women to work outside the home:

* absence of childcare facilities and other support services for working parents
* negatives attitudes towards working mothers
* lack of encouragement and support for women returning to the workforce.

Support Services for Working Parents
On the face of it, there is no reason why having children should stop women from getting a job - it doesn't in other countries to the same extent. But in Ireland little attempt is made to make it easier for mothers to work outside the home. For a start, childcare facilities, important for all employed mothers but crucial for lone parents, are limited. Only 35% of all children under the age of six are provided for in services outside the home, and three-quarters of these are in primary school.(47) In all, only 35,000 children or 9% of all the under sixes are in a service other than school, mainly in private play groups. State provision is virtually non-existent - less than 2% of children under the age of six are in a state-funded nursery activity (funded mainly through the health boards). So, child care is almost entirely in the private sector, much of it black market. Charges are uncontrolled and are likely to be beyond the budget of women on low incomes. We know virtually nothing about the numbers of children being cared for in private homes or the quality of the care they are receiving, since there is no official registration of child-minding facilities.

Workplace crèches are a rarity - only nine are known to exist in the whole country. There are five in the third-level education sector and four in large service companies. Only about 240 Irish children are known to be cared for in workplace crèches. A further barrier to women's employment is in the tax system. There is no tax relief for childcare expenses - an additional incentive for a woman to give up her job, especially if she has a second child. This is a serious gap given the high cost of childcare. With high costs and generally low wages, many women find that it is not worth their while financially to work outside the home. Other supports for women parents are also necessary, maternity leave for instance. While Irish women were given a statutory right in 1981 to pregnancy leave and job security on becoming mothers, the financial compensation (70% of earnings) is among the lowest in Europe - most European women receive their full wages while on maternity leave. An additional aid to working parents is parental leave - Ireland, Britain and Holland are the only three EC countries with no provision for parental leave. Among other helpful supports for employed mothers are flexible hours of work, job sharing, career breaks — all still scarce in Ireland.

Attitudes to Employed Mothers
Although there is more support now for a broader role for women, the motherhood role is still highly valued here. The Constitution, for instance, places the family as the 'natural primary and fundamental unit group of Society' and pledges that the state will try to ensure that women will not be forced by economic necessity to take up paid work. Some public attitudes still reflect such a traditional view of women: almost half of the people surveyed in Dublin and some rural areas in 1986 believed that women who did not want at least one child were selfish.(48) Men's attitudes are more traditional but the most conservative attitudes of all are held by people from low income backgrounds. This means that mothers from poor communities are likely to have to face many negative attitudes, along with other difficulties, should they try to take up a job.

The idea of mothers working outside the home is still not universally supported here: 46% of Irish people believe that it is bad for young children if their mother goes out to work and over a third are of the view that women should be more concerned with housekeeping and bringing up their children than with a career. This same report comments:

> *Men are still more traditional than women in their perceptions about appropriate gender role behaviour, ie they are more likely to see a woman's role as in the home and the man's outside the home. They are also more likely to see women as dependent, and to believe that the wife and mother role is the most fulfilling one women could want.(49)*

However, women themselves, also in quite large numbers, believe that mothers should not be employed while their children are young. This can lead to guilt among employed mothers and heighten ambivalence about taking up a job among mothers who are not employed.

Supports for Women Coming Back into the Workplace
Working long-term in the home isolates women from the job market. Skills become redundant, it is difficult to find potential areas of work, confidence in seeking work drops. This happens to the unemployed generally as well as women in particular but working in the home is especially isolating and often lessens women's self-esteem. Women returning to work may encounter age discrimination as well. So, one of women's greatest needs is for training and development if they are to re-enter employment. FÁS, the national training agency, runs a small number of courses for women returning to the workforce. However, these courses are just a fraction of total FÁS training activity. Since they were not widely advertised in the past, women on low incomes were less likely to hear of them. Apart from this, women may experience difficulty in getting involved in other work-related activities. The Social Employment Scheme (SES), for instance, which provides work on a half-time basis for social welfare claimants, requires that people be registered for at least a year at the employment exchange. Women have less chance of getting on this and other schemes because they tend not to register themselves as unemployed. And those on the 'women's schemes' ('deserted wife's', 'unmarried mother's' and so on) are totally excluded from these activities.

Clearly then, the fact that so much of women's work is unpaid contributes in a major way to keeping women poor. But this is not the only link between women's work and poverty: when they do work outside the home women earn less and do not fare as well as men.

PAID WORK: CREATING POVERTY FOR SOME WOMEN
Apart from the 53% of Irish women who have no income of their own, many women who do have a job are frequently badly paid. Men still earn much more than women. At the end of 1987, the average gross *weekly* pay of women in industry

was 40% below the average male wage: £139.89 as compared with £232.45 a week. This means that a woman in an industrial job would have to work a further 25 hours a week to earn the equivalent of a man's wages. Women's *hourly* earnings are a bit closer to those of men: 67.9% in 1988. Twenty years ago, in 1968, women's earnings were roughly half of men's. So, the equal pay legislation has had a limited effect, showing that legislation is only one way of dealing with the problem of sex segregation of work. Unless women can take up different types of jobs, their earnings, relative to those of men, will not significantly improve.

Irish women's earnings compare badly with those of women elsewhere. In 1986, of all EC countries, Ireland had the biggest gap between the earnings of women and men industrial manual workers, apart from Luxembourg and Britain. Danish and Italian women were at the top of the league, earning 85.9% and 84.4% of men's hourly earnings respectively.

Women start their work careers being paid similarly even slightly more than men. In 1987 the average weekly earnings of girls who had left school a year earlier were £71.80 compared with £69.30 for men.(50) This is due in part to the low wages paid to apprentices, most of whom are men. However, women soon lose their early advantage since their earnings do not increase with age as much as those of men. Women's earnings peak earlier - between 25 and 34 years of age, whereas men in industrial jobs earn their highest wages between the ages of 35 and 54. So, over the life cycle, women do not do as well from employment as men which increases their risk of poverty.

Why is it that women are paid less than men? There is no one reason for this, although the following five factors are all very significant:

* *Women work in very different kinds of jobs to men, often those that are low-paying*
* *Women do not advance up the hierarchy as quickly as men*
* *Women's family responsibilities may hold back their careers*
* *Women work for fewer hours than men*
* *Women still suffer discrimination*

43

Women Are in Different Jobs to Men

In 1987 just about a third of women were in the labour force (ie in employment or seeking work). Most women are in service jobs: nearly four-fifths of women were employed to provide services for other people in 1987. The proportion was two-thirds in 1971. Meanwhile, the numbers of women in both agriculture and industry are dropping: now just 3% of women work in the agricultural sector while 19% are in industry. The contrast with men is stark: services - 48%; agriculture - 21%; industry - 32%. Men's work situation has also changed over the last sixteen years: the numbers in agriculture continued to decline while those in service type jobs increased. Also, of course, there has been a big rise in unemployment - for both women and men.

Women dominate the sectors where wages are lowest. Service jobs among women are distinguished by their lower pay and poorer working conditions. There is more than this to sex segregation however: within each sector women do only certain types of jobs - mainly professional jobs (teaching, nursing), commercial-type work and jobs which involve providing personal services for other people. In all, 60% of women work in these three general types of job. To put names on some of the jobs women do: they are shop assistants and bar staff (31,800); professional and technical workers (89,700); clerical workers (96,200); service workers (54,000). When in industry, women work mainly in textiles, clothing and footwear - areas traditionally associated with women.

Nearly half of all women working in both industry and distribution were on low pay (ie earning less than £65 a week) in 1979, compared with 13% and 18.5% of male workers in industry and distribution.(51) Those in industry are the worst paid of all: over 70% of all low paid women workers in 1979 were working in industrial jobs. The earnings gap is largest at the lower levels.

In truth then, there has been no revolution in women's employment, apart from the fact that married women are working outside the home in larger numbers than before. The jobs they do are generally low level and low paying. Because there is very little movement of women into new areas of work, the sex structure of employment has remained largely unchanged. 'Women's jobs' and 'men's jobs' still exist and women work mainly with other women. In textiles, clothing and footwear for instance, 58% of the workers are female; in professional services nearly 60% of the workers are women; and in personal services women make up 63% of all workers. Because of this segregation, women may not always recognise discrimination - when they compare themselves with their colleagues (mostly women) they may appear to be doing well but they cannot know how they compare with men. Apart from the pay, there is another strong connection between women's employment and domestic work: the type of work involved in 'women's jobs' is often 'caring' in nature (nursing, teaching) or providing for people's personal needs (hairdressing, catering).

Women Are Not Advancing up the Jobs Hierarchy
Usually the more senior the job the more it pays. The labour market is segregated vertically as well as horizontally and men dominate the top positions. Although more women are employed now, they are not making their way to the top jobs. Women professionals, for instance, are mainly in the so-called lower professions such as teachers and nurses, whereas men dominate the better-paying professions such as accountancy, medicine, dentistry. Generally, whatever hierarchy we examine, women are likely to be at the bottom with men at the top. Take the health services for example. Over 70% of the workers are women but men hold 70% of the top positions.(52) Such low level 'crowding' of women is clearly a major reason for the poverty of households headed by a woman.

It is not only Irish women who have difficulty improving their employment position. Sex segregation in work applies with 'amazing uniformity' in the industrialised world.(53) In each of the twenty-four most developed western countries in 1980, for example, women were concentrated in clerical and service jobs. Even in Sweden, which has a very strong commitment to women's equality, the workforce remains very segregated, with 80% of women in just thirty types of job.(54)

Women's Family Responsibilities
Women enter and participate in the labour market as existing or future wives and mothers, unlike men who are workers

first and last. This difference is crucial, both on the part of workers themselves and for the way they are treated. Women's family responsibilities impinge on their work in many ways. First, employed mothers can have less time available for the job - to do overtime, to participate in educational courses outside of work, even to devote the time necessary to develop social contacts and networks - so important in many jobs today. *Work in the home is still mainly a woman's responsibility whether she is employed or not.* Husbands of employed women spend only about 4 more hours a week on housework than men whose wives are full-time in the home - 16 as against 12 hours a week.(55) So, if a woman goes out to work, she usually still retains the responsibility for home and family and the very heavy workloads associated with both. The average employed married woman in Ireland puts in a 70 hour week between home and job, compared with a 60 hour week on average for men.(56) The typical working week for the woman in the home is about 68 hours.

Women's employment careers are also interrupted for child-bearing and child-rearing. At best, they are out of their jobs for a few years. This may not seem a lot but women are often away from their jobs during the time that is most important for career advancement, the late twenties, early thirties. So, their family responsibilities are a major source of disadvantage to women in the workplace, given the present structure of work in our society.

Women are Employed for Fewer Hours than Men
According to the 1987 *Labour Force Survey*, women spend an average of 38 hours a week on the job while the average man works a 47 hour week. This explains some of the difference in earnings. Another factor is women's fairly high involvement in part-time work. Almost one in five women workers works part-time, usually paid less and in poorer conditions than full-time jobs. Women held 78% of the 96,800 part-time jobs in Ireland in 1987. In fact, this kind of work is becoming more and more important for women. In contrast, just 2% of men work in a part-time capacity, usually young and single men. Two industries predominate for part-

time work: professional services (ie education, health, legal services, etc); and a group consisting of distributive trades, insurance, finance and business services.(57) Most (63%) part-time women workers are married, so it is mainly women involved in rearing families, or those who have already done so, who work on a part-time basis. Whether women work part-time by choice or not is far from certain. One thing we can be sure of: part-time work has many disadvantages that may heighten women's risk of poverty in the long run.

Part-time jobs are paid at a lower rate - £1 to £2 an hour is not uncommon. Part-time workers are among the worst paid in the labour force and women part-timers earn least of all. This stems from a number of facts such as: many part-timers work in industries which are traditionally poorly paid; part-timers are mainly concentrated in manual occupations which are not defined as skilled, and they are in the lower grades; part-timers do not as a rule receive overtime payments; their hours are often limited and rates of pay are not covered by legislation.(58)

As well as the low earnings, the expansion of part-time work has other negative consequences. The low number of hours worked excludes many workers from legislative protection. You have to work at least eighteen hours a week to be covered for illness, redundancy, pension, maternity leave. On the basis of the *Labour Force Survey of 1987*, nearly 30,000 people worked less than eighteen hours a week, 23,000 of whom were women. Employers' costs are substantially reduced when workers are not covered by legislative protection: their PRSI contribution is lower, among other things. So, there is an incentive for employers to push their workers' hours below the statutory minimum: small wonder, then, that the hours worked by part-timers are decreasing.

Another disadvantage of part-time work is that it rarely offers any opportunities for career advancement and promotion, developing new skills or training. In addition, working conditions are often very poor in part-time jobs: cleaning work, for instance, involves very heavy workloads, unsocial hours and little work satisfaction.(59) Most part-time workers are excluded from pension schemes and they will receive sick pay only if they work more than 18 hours a week.

Discriminatory Attitudes and Practices Still Exist in Ireland

Women themselves judge the extent of sex discrimination at work to have increased over the last ten years. Substantial numbers of women say that they are being discriminated against in relation to recruitment, promotion and pay.(60) Married women particularly report more discrimination, and women on low incomes feel especially discriminated against in the quality or type of work they are asked to do. Other groups in the population, especially married men, identify far more widespread barriers to women's advancement than do women themselves. Men also identify different barriers: particularly the attitudes of management to women, lack of flexible hours and the lack of social supports for employed women.

What About the Future?

Women's disadvantage at work cannot be seen in isolation from developments in the rest of the economy. The structure of the labour force itself is changing in the search for greater profits. Employers increasingly want a flexible and cheaper labour force. Women, as the weaker sector of the employed, are very vulnerable to higher unemployment and other changes such as increasing technology and job deskilling.

Today almost a quarter of a million people are unemployed in the Republic, although the rate of increase has slowed down, mainly because so many people are emigrating. Usually thought of as a man's problem, women are increasingly affected by unemployment - 70,424 women were registered as unemployed in November 1988 (ie signing on the Live Register as available for work). At this time, some 163,896 men were on the Live Register. According to the latest *Labour Force Survey*, 14% of women in the labour force were unemployed or seeking their first regular job in mid-1987, over a quarter of whom were under 25 years of age. Both the absolute numbers of women and the rate of women's unemployment are increasing all the time. *In fact, women's rate of unemployment has almost tripled since 1971: from 5% to 14%.*

Unemployment among Irish women differs in a number of ways from that of men. The official rate of female unemployment is lower than the rate for men: 14% as against 19%, but this difference may be more apparent than real, since unemployment statistics need to be treated cautiously, especially those for women. The Live Register (compiled at the Employment Exchanges) underestimates the 'true' rate of women's unemployment because many women do not bother to sign on as they are not eligible for benefit (mainly because their husbands are claiming means-tested unemployment assistance for the family). Also, women cannot sign on if they are available only for part-time work.(61) In addition, women may be more likely than men to become discouraged and to withdraw from the search for work, giving in to pressure to remain in their traditional roles. While the social welfare changes introduced for the implementation of the EC equality directive in 1986 have reduced the extent to which the Live Register undercounts women, *an unknown number of unemployed women still go unnoticed and unrecorded.*

A lower rate of women's unemployment makes us very unusual internationally. Among our EC neighbours we share this only with Britain and Holland. In other countries, women have been more affected than men by unemployment: in 1982 the OECD Observer reported 'those people hardest hit are those whose supply has expanded most rapidly - youth and women'.(62)

Women are disadvantaged in the new and developing industries as well. Take electronics for instance - one of the most dynamic sectors today. A survey of the electronics industry found that only 3% of all managers and 15% of all professionals were women, while they comprised over 70% of all assembly workers.(63) This is very entrenched segregation in such a young industry. Women were disadvantaged because they did not have the right (technical) qualifications to begin with, and once in the firm they received only a very limited type of training and were not promoted as readily as men. Developments like the increased computerisation of white collar occupations and the decline of mass industries do not bode well for women's employment. Women will probably face greater competition for the jobs that they have traditionally done from redundant and unemployed male workers and young men seeking their first job.

What are the chances of breaking down segregation? There is certainly cause for pessimism, given that the equality legislation appears to have reached the limits of its effectiveness. And of course, legislation alone cannot end segregation. Positive action programmes are also needed to encourage and train women to enter new spheres of activity, while at the same time attacking the negative attitudes and prejudices that exist about women working. It must also be made easier for women to work outside the home, if that is their wish. Vital support services for working parents, like crèches and other childcare arrangements, flexible working times and parental leave, are not widely available in Ireland. Childcare especially can be very expensive.

Low pay continues to be a major problem: significant numbers of women are in low paying, low level jobs and this means that *work can contribute to women's poverty rather than end it*. So, unless something is done about the wage rates paid by employers to employees, and especially women employees, women will continue to be poor as workers.

THE SELF DESTRUCTION OF JENNY RICE

Moira Stowe

I know a girl named Jenny Rice
Who bought a house in Paradise
Picasso prints adorned her walls
And musical chimes chimed in the hall
When someone rang the doorbell.

She filled that house with china dogs
Crinoline ladies and porcelain frogs
All polished till they shone and gleamed
At night she went to bed and dreamed
Of more.

No human ever crossed her door
(For fear that they might soil the floor)
So people left her to herself
To contemplate the ornaments
that sparkled on her shelf.

The years passed by and Jenny stayed
Within the prison she had made
Secure from all the joy and strife
That constitute the pace and pulse of life.

One day a great big crack appeared
In Jenny Rice's armour
'Neurosis' said the Doctor
He prescribed some pills to calm her
And they did.

Now Jenny mostly sits and broods
The magic pills control her moods
The pill box states 'Take One Pill Only'
In truth it really says
'Jenny's lonely'.

First published in *Notions*. Dublin: Klear/Borderline, 1987.

WOMEN, SOCIAL WELFARE AND POVERTY

Despite its occasional claims to the contrary, one of the foremost purposes of the social security system in its dealings with women is wherever possible to relieve itself of any responsibility for their support and maintenance, and leave them financially dependent upon the resources of husbands, lovers or friends.(64)

Nearly half a million women in Ireland now depend on social welfare.(65) When all the women, men and children on welfare are added together the total comes to over 1.3 million people - 37% of the population. For women social welfare is even more important than it is for men - as many women rely on it directly as have a job. There is also a sizable group of women on whose behalf men claim social welfare. Yet the system is planned mainly by men and with the life patterns of men in mind. In the process of providing payments, social welfare treats people in certain ways and reinforces values and behaviours that are linked to poverty. So the social welfare system has major effects on women as individuals and on women's role in society generally.

There are two crucial factors which link social welfare and poverty among women:

* large numbers of women are existing on low payments
* being on social welfare reinforces women's dependency over time and therefore contributes to their long-term poverty.

EXISTING ON LOW PAYMENTS

More and more women are relying on social welfare as the years go by - the numbers grew by 90% over the last ten years to reach almost a half a million in 1987.(66) Unemployment was the main reason for this, both because the rates soared and also because the changes in social welfare inroduced by the implementation of the EC equality directive in 1986, and in compliance with the judgements in some constitutional cases, made more women eligible for unemployment payments. Before this, unemployed married women had very limited entitlement to social welfare. Other women are also relying more on welfare now: the numbers on 'deserted wife's', 'unmarried mothers' and all other 'women's schemes' have grown by 50% over the last ten years to reach almost 130,000 today. Some of these schemes grew more than others: for example, between 1977 and 1987, the numbers on unmarried mother's allowance grew by 200%, the number of 'deserted wives' more than doubled and widowed claimants increased by a third. So, social welfare is increasingly vital to women and is an essential part of any strategy to combat poverty among women.

Table 3:
Women in the Social Welfare System in 1987

Claimants in their own right because they are unemployed, ill or elderly	210,364
Entitled to income maintenance because they are rearing children on their own and/or are without a man to maintain them	128,142
Dependants of male claimants (estimated)	125,000
TOTAL	**463,506**

(Source: Department of Social Welfare, *Statistical Information on Social Welfare Services 1987.*)

The social welfare system divides women into three main groupings:

* those receiving payments in their own right (ie old age pensioners, unemployed and ill women)
* those on 'women's schemes' ('deserted wives', 'unmarried mothers', 'single women', prisoners' wives, widows)
* women on whose behalf men are claiming social welfare

How much do these women have to live on? This is not easy

to say because they do not all receive the same amount - there are at least thirty-three social welfare schemes, many with different rates of payment. In fact, as Table 4 shows, the rates vary between £58.50 a week (for an old age contributory pensioner) and £25 a week (also for a pensioner but this time for the spouse of a non-contributory pensioner). Women working full time in the home are among the worst off - their husbands claim for them but the amount is small. On the basis of 1987 figures, an estimated 125,000 women get less than £30 a week or, to to be precise, their husbands get this amount of money from social welfare for them each week. A woman rearing a family on her own gets about £49 for herself and between £10 and £15 for each child.

Over time, the value of social welfare has been kept in line with inflation, and some payments have been increased substantially. However, the payment base was very low to begin with, so many social welfare payments are now inadequate. Generally, people seem to be able to manage the basics, but when they have a large occasional expense, such as a birth or death in the family or even a large electricity bill in winter, they run into debt.(67) Practically all welfare payments are still below the minimum recommended by the Commission on Social Welfare - in today's values between £55 and £65 a week for an individual, around £96 for a couple. Now if we consider the costs associated with children, the only group for whom there is specific evidence, we discover, according to estimates for 1987, that children cost the following amounts a week to rear (68):

one child under four years	£19.60
one child over four years	£28.20
two children under four years	£24.30
two children over four years	£44.40

And yet the highest social welfare payment for a child is around £14 a week, and £10 is the most common payment. Parents are not helped by the fact that the rates for children do not increase as they get older.

So, clearly, there is a problem with low social welfare payment levels. Why are they so low? Budgetary constraints are one reason: each year social welfare increases in the

Budget depend on how much the government is prepared to spend, rather than on how much money people need. Payment rates have never been worked out on the basis of need and there is no official poverty line in Ireland. It is not clear even if the social welfare system works on the basis of a specific view of poverty - the elimination of poverty has never been stated as a particular aim of social welfare policy. It would appear to view poverty in an absolute way - it occurs when people cannot afford to feed, clothe and get basic accommodation for themselves. This view justifies social welfare meeting only basic needs.

However, ending poverty would require significant redistribution of resources, wealth and opportunities across the population. Although social welfare does redistribute income in a small way, it does not shift enough income, opportunities and other resources to those who are poor. Since it is only part of the state's financial structure, it is probably unrealistic to expect social welfare to eliminate poverty by itself. However, it could be expected to maintain people at a reasonable standard of living. At current rates of payment, social welfare fails to do this. As well as higher payment rates, the transition from welfare to a job should be easier if poverty is to be eliminated. At present, some welfare payments are cut very severely when someone has part-time earnings. The exceptions to this are the 200 people on the part-time job incentive scheme - a scheme allowing a person who is long-term unemployed to work a maximum of twenty-four hours a week, while receiving a weekly social welfare payment of around £27. Education, one of the best routes to paid work, is denied to all but a small number of unemployed claimants. Another barrier to people working is the fact that when they take up a job they may lose other benefits such as a medical card and their differential local authority rent may increase. This is part of the 'poverty trap'.

THE LONG-TERM CONSEQUENCES OF SOCIAL WELFARE FOR WOMEN

There is also a second link between social welfare and poverty - its long-term consequences. Being on social welfare for a long period of time affects people and their place in society. There are several especially damaging consequences for women. Over time, social welfare:

* reproduces traditional divisions between women and men
* prolongs women's dependency
* increases hardship for women
* leads to differences between women claimants
* excludes some women from specific social welfare coverage

Each of these consequences comes about in a particular way.

1. Reproducing Sex Role Divisions

Even though it is possible to argue from a legal point of view that there is equal treatment since the equality directive in 1986, in practice the consequences of social welfare are different for women and men because they take different routes into the system and therefore often find themselves on different schemes. Women enter social welfare either as lone parents, as men's dependants or as claimants in their own right. Men are almost exclusively individual claimants. So, while it is true that the equality directive removed the grosser forms of discrimination, the circumstances of women and men on social welfare still vary because their life patterns are different.

To begin with, fewer men have to depend on social welfare: an estimated 400,000 as against 463,000 women in 1987. Secondly, most men claim in their own right and, if relevant, for their families, which means that they usually receive the full adult payment for themselves, as well as the dependent spouse part for their partners without question. In effect then, men as a group receive higher payments than women and more men receive a payment directly - there are four women adult dependants (on an average payment of £29 a week) for every one male adult dependant. This also, of course, means that men are guaranteed their payment, whereas at least 125,000 women have to wait for their husbands to hand over their share. Thirdly, men are not put through the very personal investigation process which women applicants often have to undergo to establish whether they really are 'deserted', 'unmarried', not cohabiting, and so on. Finally, although there is about the same proportion of men and women on the higher level benefit payments, some categories of women are more likely to be on assistance payments. This is especially true of old age pensioners: 68% of women compared with 39% of men are on non-contributory old age pensions. This can mean a significant difference in income - contributory pensioners are paid about £8.50 more a week (or 17%). Thus, women's risk of poverty in old age is increased.

2. Prolonging Women's Dependency

More and more women are having to rely on social welfare - the numer of women on unemployment payments alone increased by 600% over the last ten years. Most women relate to social welfare as mothers or non-mothers, or 'wives' or 'non-wives'. The schemes are even titled to denote a woman's marital status: 'widow', 'deserted wife', 'prisoner's wife', 'unmarried mother', 'single woman'. Up to this year, such schemes had no parallel among men - schemes for deserted husbands and widowers are now being introduced. Women on these schemes are not expected to be paid workers and there is no encouragement for them to enter the labour market - which would give them a better chance of an adequate income. Social welfare still finds it very difficult to accommodate women in a number of roles. While enough money is provided to ward off destitution, as the system is currently organised and given existing levels of payment, it does nothing to prevent long-term dependence for women.

Even if it did not actively encourage them to rejoin the labour market, social welfare could certainly reduce women's dependency by giving both partners equal payments. Yet, any woman married to a man claiming social welfare (and from now on this applies to women living with men as well) is automatically considered his dependant and the payment is a joint one. There are an estimated 125,000 women classified like this in the social welfare system and about 30,000 men at most. These women are married mainly to unemployed or ill men, all are working full time in the home, most caring for children. Not receiving a payment of their own means that they have to depend for their weekly money on men, some of whom may be unreliable in handing over enough for the household. So, women's direct access to money is reduced which can lead to financial hardship. The practice of payments for adult dependants also reinforces traditional power relationships between men and women: because men get the money they retain the power over it, just as they would with wages. Although technically a woman can now claim a payment for the family, her husband must first agree. In practice very few women do and they are unlikely to do so in the future because it goes against the norm. In any case, the notion of dependency in marriage is unchanged since one spouse still has to be treated as the dependant of the other. There is no economic reason why each partner should not get an equal individual payment.

The notion of dependency in social welfare has recently been reinforced by the government's response to the Supreme Court's ruling (in the Hyland case) that social welfare's treatment of married couples, following the EC equality directive, was unconstitutional. An estimated 8,000 married couples where both partners are on a welfare payment receive about £14 a week less than an unmarried couple in the same situation. In response to the ruling, the government has decided to 'equalise' downwards: to reduce the entitlement of cohabiting couples by £14 a week, rather than to raise a married couple's payment by that amount. So, the assumption of dependency in marriage continues unchallenged and it is now extended to unmarried couples as well. A situation where all single dole claimants will be interrogated about their private lives and living arrangements now seems certain.

What does it mean to be a dependant? If assigned this status, the social welfare system considers that you need less money: the payment for the 'dependent spouse' is only around 60% of that for the main claimant.(69) Two people may be able to live more cheaply than one but why is it that the cheaper payment is most often for the woman? Also, why aren't the same dependency rules applied to *any* two people forming a household?

'Split payments' provide one of the clearest examples of the hardship and discrimination that arise from the assumption of dependency. Sheila had great trouble getting money from her husband, even when he was employed the entire family income was frequently spent by him on alcohol. She heard from a neighbour that it was possible to get her share (ie the adult dependant's allowance), as well as the children's allowance, paid separately from her husband.(70) After a long time, she succeeded - first she had difficulty finding out how to arrange it and then it took her a long time to persuade her husband to agree. She was disappointed to discover that the split was not 50/50 however: even though she is responsible for the running of the household, she can only receive the smaller share. Sheila currently gets £29 for herself while her husband's personal payment a week is £47, most of which he still spends on alcohol. And out of her share she has to meet the *family's* commitments on rent, electricity, fuel, food and all the other expenses. No one knows exactly how many women are in Sheila's position because there are no published statistics, not even an official title or term exists for the arrangement. Estimates by the Department of Social Welfare put the number of women in this situation at around 4,500. The Department has announced an intention to change this arrangement, exactly how is not yet known.

3. Creating Hardship for Women

How do you contact a 'deserting' husband for evidence that he left by his own wish? How do you even trace a deserting husband? These are some ways in which the conditions attaching to 'women's schemes' can be difficult, even impossible, to satisfy. They also invade women's private lives.

Joan's efforts to join the 12,000 women on the deserted wife's scheme is a typical case. When her husband left, after years of violence and threats, full responsibility was placed on Joan for both tracing him and obtaining maintenance from him. When she went to the community welfare officer she was told that she could get a temporary payment for a time; to qualify for the deserted wife's allowance she would have to: (a) be 'deserted' for three months; (b) not be in receipt of adequate maintenance from her husband; (c) prove that she had made 'reasonable efforts' to obtain maintenance from him; d) be aged over 40 years if she had no dependent children; (e) not be living with another man. Where should she start? The first thing she had to do was to notify the Gardai - she was then 'officially' deserted. Next, to prove that she had made 'reasonable efforts' to trace him, she had to go to her husband's family to try and find out if they knew where he was, terrified that she would actually find him given his violent nature. They were not helpful, blaming her for the break-up. She felt even more degraded by having to approach a local priest for a letter 'proving' that she was deserted. She also had to issue a summons for maintenance since he had a job. All of this at a time when she was very vulnerable, and each week she had to queue, sometimes for two hours or more, at the local health centre to get her temporary payment. Joan, as it turned out, was one of the lucky ones - she was accepted for deserted wife's benefit. Recent research found that only 57% of a sample of applicants for 'deserted wife's' payments succeeded.(71) Equally, had her husband been suspected of being in Britain, Joan would have had to contact the DHSS in Newcastle-upon-Tyne inquiring about his whereabouts. In all, it took nearly six months before her payment came through. What struck Joan forcibly was how little the state did to seek out her husband, and presumably other husbands, largely ignoring the possibility of recouping some of the money from them.(72) While she appreciates the payment because it is secure and gives her her own money for the first time in her life, Joan wonders why she has to be called a 'deserted wife', which she finds so degrading.

One of the main conditions for 'desertion' - that the man left voluntarily - requires a woman to be a passive victim before she can qualify for the scheme. In effect, there are no limits on why the husband may leave, so he has a more legitimate right to break up a marriage, while a woman must be forced to leave him, mainly because of the threat of violence - and even this element of constructive desertion is very recent. Apart from the questionable values underlying them, the conditions can also compel women to remain in marriages which are intolerable.

In general, given the conditions attaching to 'women's schemes', the enquiry process preceding payment intrudes into deeply personal areas of a woman's life, at a time which may be very painful for her. The difficulty of satisfying the conditions and their lack of clarity gives immense power to the individual social welfare official. The cohabitation rule (ie the need to ensure that a claimant is not cohabiting) is notorious in this context. Although in principle it applies equally to men's schemes, far more women than men are subjected to its invasive interrogation process. Women's homes are known to be inspected for evidence of a man's presence. One woman tells how she had a visit from a social welfare officer early one morning because a car was parked in her driveway overnight. It was not easy to convince him that it belonged to her brother-in-law and was there because it had broken down. If evidence is found of a man's presence in the home, a woman's payment is in jeopardy. In applying the cohabitation rule a number of highly questionable assumptions are often made: first, that if a man is on the premises they are sleeping together; secondly that he therefore must maintain her. There are overtones of prostitution in this, which reveal a belief at the heart of social welfare - *that women have no fundamental right to maintenance from the state if they are in a sexual relationship with a man.* So, for many women, being on social welfare reduces their choice about relationships with men - effectively those on 'women's schemes' cannot have a close relationship with a man if they want to retain their current level of social welfare.

4. Treating Women Differently

The fact that they are separated into different categories on the basis of their marital and family status has led to women being treated differently. Women in quite similar circumstances receive different amounts of money depending on which scheme they are in. Compare the rates paid to and for women across social welfare schemes in 1989 (see table 4).

At least ten different economic values are placed on women (73), most of whom are doing the same work: caring for homes and children. These values range from a high of £58.50 a week (for an old age contributory pensioner) to a low of £25.10 (for a dependant of an old age non-contributory pensioner). While some of these rates apply to men as well as women, there are four times as many women adult dependants. So, the rates paid for dependants can reasonably be regarded as the state's estimate of the worth of women working in the home.

Table 4:
Variations in the Amounts Paid Per Week to/for a Woman on Social Welfare

	Benefit/ Contributory	Assistance/ Non-contributory
Unemployed woman*	£45.00	£47.00
Old age pensioner**	£58.50	£50.00
Widow/Deserted Wife**	£52.50	£49.00
Unmarried Mother/ Prisoner's Wife	—	£49.00
Single Woman's Allowance	—	£47.00
Dependant of Unemployed Man (for less than 15 months)*	£29.00	£26.90
Dependant of Unemployed Man (for more than 15 months)*		£29.00
Dependant of Old Age Pensioner	£37.30	£25.10

* these are the rates for male and female urban claimants. In the case of the wife of an unemployed man she is claimed for as his dependant. The assistance rate cited for the unemployed woman is the long-term (ie over 15 months) rate.
** these rates are for widows and deserted wives aged under 66 years and for old age pensioners aged under 80 years.

It would appear that some women have a higher monetary value than others: at the top of the hierarchy are old age pensioners and widows; at the bottom are women married to unemployed men and pensioners, entitled to only between £25 and £29 a week.(74) The size of the gap between the amounts paid for women treated as men's dependants and other women is enormous: in some cases more than half. Given the organisation of the social welfare system, then, women are financially better off without a man, except when they reach old age. Such variation in rates creates inequalities amongst women, placing some in a position of relative advantage over others. While insurance and assistance rates have always differed, it is impossible to justify the three different rates paid to women for their own up-keep within insurance and assistance schemes.

5. Excluding Some Women from Social Welfare
Furthermore, there are women who do not qualify under any

specific scheme. For instance, those whose marriages have broken down for reasons other than desertion may have difficulty qualifying for a specific payment. The 'deserted wife's' payment is limited by a very strict definition of what constitutes desertion: a woman is considered to be 'deserted' when her husband leaves voluntarily or she has to leave him. Clearly, social welfare makes no specific provision for women who are separated, divorced and living apart from their husbands for reasons other than desertion. Not catered for either are women who cannot prove that their husbands left voluntarily or that they had to leave him. Similarly, there is no specific social welfare scheme for women married to men serving prison sentences of less than six months. Women in these situations are forced to rely on the supplementary welfare allowance - the safety net scheme with the lowest rates of payment.

Many women, especially those who are married and caring for elderly and ill relatives, are also largely excluded from benefits. Take the case of Maura for instance. Her mother is one of the 66,000 elderly estimated to be cared for at home, 80% of them by women. Yet Maura is one of only around 2,000 people for whom the prescribed relative's allowance is paid. Maura gave up her job three years ago to care full time for her mother, moving back to her home town from Dublin. She now has no source of independent income of her own. She is lucky to qualify since very strict conditions apply, both for the carer and the person receiving care. The incapacitated person must usually be over 66 years of age, be already in receipt of the care to be paid for and be living alone except for the caring relative (or a dependent child or handicapped person). This is not all: only a close relative is eligible to be the carer and they must not be a married person dependent on spouse and/or working outside the home. It took Maura a long time to persuade her mother to claim - she considered it Maura's duty to care for her and was suspicious of the allowance. So Maura is actually grateful for the £28 a week, even though it is totally inadequate and, until recently, she had to receive it from her mother. The reality is that Maura's situation is likely to go on for a while yet - the average carer spends up to six years in this role.(75) Maura gets little help from the authorities -

a common experience among carers according to research. She cannot leave her mother for more than an hour at a time, and a holiday or even a short break is out of the question, even if she could afford it. And yet if she did not care for her mother, it would cost the state up to £200 a week to keep her mother in institutional care. Were Maura married, she would be unlikely to get the allowance. The condition that married women can claim only if they are not being provided for by their husbands presumably reflects the belief that these women would be caring anyway so why pay them unless one has to!

Such gaps in provision seriously question whether the social welfare system is able to cope with the changing nature of women's (and men's) lives. A single scheme for all lone parents, both male and female, should be introduced along with adequate provision for carers. These would get rid of the gaps in providing for women and also some of the inequalities in the social welfare system.

A System Designed by Men for Men

Originating in Germany and Britain at the beginning of this century when employment was fairly widespread, the social welfare system is designed around a traditional model of a man's working life. Many of its assumptions still come from that model - that unemployment is unusual in a man's working career and is short term, that the elderly and children will be cared for by women at home, that married women do not need an income of their own and can survive on less money.(76) But women's lives do not follow the same patterns as men, and, in any case, a single job for life is no longer true for men. For a start, women's employment careers are either shorter than men's or are more frequently interrupted. And, women's work is different, being based mainly in the home and, if waged, often being low paid and/or part-time. So, a system based on social insurance contributions cannot make proper provision for women who are not normally in work that is insured. The social welfare system has not come to terms with this: work in the home is not covered for social insurance, nor is part-time work for less than 18 hours a week fully covered. Maternity, a major 'risk' to women's earning capacity, is only provided for in a limited way. So women's needs and their life patterns were peripheral to the original design of the social welfare system and since then have been considered mainly when they could no longer be overlooked, as with the equality directive which was imposed by the EC.

Patriarchal Values Underlying Social Welfare

It is tempting to regard social welfare just as a set of incrementalist schemes. Even from this view, it is an extremely complex system - with at least thirty-three different schemes - making it very difficult for people to find their way around. But social welfare is more than a set of schemes: it embodies beliefs about rights and duties in society and in marriage, about the family and the roles of women and men. Social welfare officials in following regulations are putting the state's policies and values into practice. This often involves making judgements about who is 'deserving' of welfare and how much they should get. In a sense, the worth of people is being judged - different amounts are paid depending on which of the many schemes one is in. In deciding how much people should be paid and who should get paid the most, the social welfare system reflects and reinforces values operating in society as a whole.

While it may be an overstatement to claim that the social welfare system has a coherent policy on women, its core values do fundamentally affect women. Two of these are central: women should be financially supported by men, and the traditional family with the man as the breadwinner must be protected. Each of these has consequences for women: the first perpetuates women as men's dependants; the second prolongs a traditional home-making role for women.

The protection of the traditional family is fundamental to social welfare and this is why women are treated as men's dependants. Social welfare payments are family-centred, modelled on the notion of the family wage - hence one payment is usually made for the entire family and that for the adult dependant is around 60% of the main payment, perhaps because this is roughly what women earn as a proportion of men's earnings. Social welfare defines the family as that based on marriage with men as breadwinners. Millar shows what this means:

Family needs are addressed in current income
support policies on the basis of an underlying
model of the family which assumes a clear
separation of the two main functions of the family
with regard to children - the caring function being
the province of the mother and the providing
function the province of the father.(77)

Whether this is for moral reasons or not, there is certainly an economic dimension to it. Think of the enormous expense to the state if the traditional model of the family (in which a woman working full-time in the home is essential) did not operate - the costs of caring for children, the ill and the elderly would soar, as would the state's bill for women's social welfare. In an important sense, the relationship between women and the state is one of interdependence: more and more women are being pushed into reliance on social welfare but, equally, the state needs women to provide the services that all wives and mothers provide. Similarly, women's relationship to social welfare is not by any means a simple one: social welfare is vitally important to women who wish or are forced to live without a man and are not in paid employment.

And yet the potential of social welfare to reduce women's dependence is not realised as we saw when we looked at its long-term consequences for women. Families that do not conform to the traditional model are treated as exceptions and are fitted in under special schemes. Most of these are families headed by women: 'deserted wives', 'unmarried mothers', widows. These families are actually paid more than others which seems at odds with the rhetoric in the Constitution. Article 41.2, pledges, among other things, that the state will endeavour to ensure that mothers shall not be 'obliged by economic necessity to engage in labour to the neglect of their duties in the home.' The reference here is not to all women but to mothers. This pledge to protect the family and women's traditional role within it is at the core of women's and men's treatment in social welfare. The rates paid to many women depend on their marital and/or motherhood status and the differences can be explained in terms of their effect on families. Given the state's concern to protect the family, widows, 'deserted wives' and other women parenting alone are paid more because, not having a man to provide for them, the welfare of their families is in their hands and, if they had to work outside the home, they might neglect their 'duties'. Women with husbands, however, are a different matter: while the social welfare system is willing to make a contribution for their upkeep, it must not interfere with a man's responsibility to provide for his spouse and family. Thus, he usually receives the payment for both of them and his is the larger share.

The failure to change this can be traced to policy makers' reluctance to tackle problems of inequalities within families. In this way, the traditional family structure is protected and a woman remains dependent on her husband. So, the state operates above all to protect family responsibilities and will intervene between a woman and her husband, and from now on between cohabiting women and men, only as a last resort.

MY ALPHABET

Mona

A is for anger which I feel a lot of
B is for bored which I sometimes feel
C is for children of which I have two
D is for drink which I sometimes do
E is for eagerness I feel now and then
F is for frustration
G is for giving it works both ways
H is for husband I only have one (Thank God)
I is for Ireland my home country
J is for jewels that I would love to own
K is for knitting which I would love to learn
L is to try to learn a lot more
M is for myself
N is for try to say 'No' more often
O is for optimistic
P is for pleasing people
Q is for quietness
R is for regrets I have a small few
S is for try to say sorry when I should
T is for trying
U is for uptight
V is for venison the meat from the deer
W is for washday
X is for Xmas which I love so much
Y is for the youth of tomorrow
Z is for the zoo where the animals live.

First published in *Womenwrite*. Dublin: Lourdes Youth and Community Training.

5

WOMEN'S ACCESS TO EDUCATION, HOUSING AND LEGAL SERVICES

*It advances our understanding of poverty to have it
described not as a set of symptoms diagnosed in
certain kinds of people (those suffering from ill-
health, old age, dark skin), but as a result of the
mechanisms that govern the distribution of national
wealth so that certain people are a priori excluded
from the race.(78)*

Another very important factor influencing quality of life is
access to public services. Such services are provided by the
state to protect citizens and improve the quality of their lives.
Education prepares people for work, housing provides
accommodation and legal services give people access to their
rights. These services are vitally important in shaping
people's lifestyle and their future life chances. Without
education, for instance, the chances of getting a well-paid job
are slim. In theory, the Irish public services guarantee the
right of access to everyone, especially those on low incomes.
In practice, however, people can slip through the net and the
quality of the service received varies.

EDUCATION

Access to Education
Education should be thought of as a resource, one of the most
valuable of all. Education gives access to better life chances,
to job opportunities, to different ways of thinking and also to
new images of ourselves. Entry to most jobs nowadays is
strictly controlled by certificates and qualifications. It is
hardly an exaggeration to liken educational institutions to job
placement agencies. This is a relatively recent role for
education: up to the 1960s family assets, such as land or a
business, had a much bigger influence on the career paths of

young people. Achievements in educational participation in Ireland have been considerable: about 60% of young people now remain in school up to the end of second-level education. However, the kind of education they receive varies very much by social class and sex.

Class Differences in Education

Class differences show themselves in many ways: for instance, in the type of school attended - children from lower income backgrounds are highly represented in vocational schools, while almost all middle class children attend secondary schools; in the age at leaving school - children from poorer backgrounds spend a shorter time in school than middle class children and many children from poorer backgrounds drop out of the school system early. Roughly about a third of girls and a half of boys never sit the Leaving Certificate examination. According to official sources, about 6,000 young people leave school each year without any qualifications, and up to 4,000 more attempt and fail to get a certificate. Boys outnumber girls here but most early leavers share one characteristic: their low income backgrounds. With about 10% of children leaving school without qualifications, it is little wonder that literacy difficulties are widespread: nearly 400,000 Irish people are estimated officially to require tuition in literacy, and the real number may be higher.(79) For the unqualified school leavers jobs are unlikely to exist since the number of unskilled jobs is falling all the time. The earlier one leaves school the greater the chances of ending up unemployed - in one study three and half times more of those who had left school without any exam were unemployed than people with a Leaving Certificate.(80) Having at least one exam halves the odds of being unemployed one year after leaving school.(81)

Although differences have lessened since 'free education' was introduced in 1967, social class differences remain. Ireland concentrated on removing financial barriers to education but true equality means two things: *equal access* to and *equal treatment* in education once within the system. Equal access does not exist here because some schools and some types of education cost more than others. As the cutbacks bite deeper, school staffing and funding are being

70

affected, especially schools in poorer areas which have difficulty raising funds privately. Examination fees are now expensive (eg £35 for the Leaving Certificate and £200 to repeat it), as are books and uniforms. Some second-level schools have introduced 'voluntary' charges. The pupil-teacher ratio is increasing, guidance and remedial services which are vital to many children from poor backgrounds are being cut back, and vocational preparation and training allowances for some students have been eliminated. These changes can only worsen the class differences in access to education. People with money can adapt by buying tuition and education privately for their children.

Nor is there equal treatment across schools because second-level education is dominated by private secondary schools which have more resources and draw their pupils from better-off backgrounds than other schools. Differences are even greater at third-level: the higher up one's parents are on the class hierarchy the greater one's chances of going to college, and especially to university. Over half of all new students at third-level in 1986 came from five social class groups (mainly the professions, employers and managers and salaried employees), and a further 20% were from farming families.(82) Only 1% of college entrants had fathers who worked in an unskilled manual job and 2.5% were from families on the next rung in the hierarchy - semi-skilled manual. Looked at over time, the education system has been a major vehicle through which privilege, and poverty, are passed on from generation to generation. The children of the better off (ie those with land and other property and the professional classes) have benefited most from increased public spending on education. The result: 'a virtual upper class monopoly of the advantages that depend on education'.(83)

Sex Differences in Education
The education received by the 60,000 girls and boys who leave second-level education each year still differs in many ways. First, more of the girls will have attended single sex and secondary schools. Although co-education is increasing, 46% of second-level schools are still single sex, and more so for girls than for boys. Attending different schools can mean a

71

different emphasis in education because so many factors vary from school to school: the choice of available subjects, the ethos of the school, the attitudes of teachers, encouragement to pursue different subjects and careers. Boys' schools in Ireland are more achievement oriented and more specialised, concentrating their seniors into one or two areas such as science and commerce.(84) Girls' schools, on the other hand, are far more likely to offer a variety of subjects, teaching some of this, some of that, although focusing on the so-called 'girls' subjects'.

This leads to a second difference between boys and girls: they study and do their examinations in quite different subjects. The 'girls' subjects'are home economics, art, music, and to some extent languages and business organisation; science (apart from biology) and the technical subjects (technical drawing, engineering, building construction) are 'boys'subjects'. In this way, girls and boys are choosing or being directed towards quite different life paths. The very general and non-technical subjects chosen by the girls steer them away from the well-paying, expanding areas of work such as computers and technology, while it is to these very areas that boys are being directed.

Girls as a group out-perform boys at second-level but this advantage is not translated into well-paying jobs and careers. Why? Part of the reason is that fewer women go on to university or other higher education colleges, even though more girls than boys complete the Leaving Certificate. In 1986 48% of new entrants to third-level education were women, even though girls make up over half of those who complete the Leaving Certificate.(85) And women go to different kinds of colleges, especially the teacher training colleges, whereas the Royal College of Surgeons, the Regional Technical Colleges and the two newest universities, Dublin City University and the University of Limerick (formerly the National Institutes for Higher Education), have far greater numbers of men. Women also pursue different courses at college: they mainly do arts, science and commerce. Only a quarter of all women entering college in 1986 were studying for the most rapidly expanding job area of all - science and technology - compared with 56% of men. These sex differences are reflected in degree patterns.

Sex differences are stronger at the lower end of the socio-economic scale. Upper class girls are more likely to have a choice of subjects and to be encouraged to go for non-traditional careers. However, girls' education is different from boys' in all social classes. Not one but a number of factors push girls towards traditional subjects. The most crucial is their own selection process: girls elect to study traditional subjects.(86) Their choice is often very limited however: schools provide certain subjects only and these are allocated in a particular way with conditions usually set by the school for studying each subject. So, the possibilities for girls to take non-traditional subjects are often limited. The notion of the 'hidden curriculum' has been used to explain how sex and other differences are reproduced in schools.(87) Schools pass on far more than just what is in the text book. In preparing for adult roles, they also shape attitudes and values and help to form self-image. Educational experience can either give self-confidence and a belief in one's own ability or it can undermine self-esteem.

Think of the average child's schooling. Her or his first experience of school, especially if from a low income family, is likely to be at primary school. Publicly funded nursery or pre-school facilities are very limited in Ireland, even though they are recognised elsewhere as a vital first step for children. In Ireland children usually only go to nursery or pre-school if their parents can pay for them. On entering primary school and certainly for the first few years, the child will be taught or 'minded' by a woman teacher - women outnumber men by three to one in the primary teaching profession, but men usually teach the higher classes. For the young child the association between mother and woman teacher is a strong one. As the child moves up through the primary school she or he will come across even more powerful role models: junior teachers will be women but senior teachers and almost all principals will be men - men are five times more likely than women to be promoted to primary school principal. So the child sees men as the authority figures. This link continues up to third-level where only 5% of the senior lecturing staff are women.(88) The message being transmitted throughout is that men have the power and make the decisions which women carry out.

The link between men and authority is reinforced in other ways as well. In school text books, for example, it has been found that: (1) women are often invisible, (2) when they do appear women are in low status or 'second rate' jobs, (3) there is an over-riding emphasis on women's domestic role.(89) School texts usually depict white, middle class lifestyles and opportunities as well. In addition, many of the subjects girls study, even if they are by their own choice, reinforce a secondary role for women. What is domestic science after all if not primarily a preparation for home and marriage?

While some change is certainly occurring, powerful conservative forces still exist. One such force is the link between catholicism and schooling. In Ireland there are no state-run schools at primary level - primary schools are privately run by an individual board of management, although totally state-funded. The catholic influence is strong in that the local parish priest or curate usually chairs the board of management in the majority of schools, and so has control over the recruitment of staff and the general running of the school. The Constitution places the state's responsibility for education third after the family and 'private and corporate educational initiative'. So the majority of secondary schools (64%) are owned and controlled by either nuns, brothers or priests, even though they are almost totally state-funded. This closely links catholic values with educational content. Such values not only inform religion classes but are also incorporated into the school ethos. Catholic values emphasise women as mothers - with Mary as the model - endorsing such values as obedience, chastity, deference and femininity. Through these and other influences, girls may acquire different academic expectations to boys, particularly in areas which are seen as the male domain - maths, science, technology. These expectations prevent girls from taking these subjects or, when they do, they may impede their performance.

Adult Education
If women want to pursue further education later on, cost can often be a barrier. Adult education courses, for instance, usually cost at least £20 - a third of the weekly income of a

woman on unmarried mother's allowance. The cost to the student is being pushed up as public spending cut-backs bite deeper - AONTAS (National Association of Adult Education) estimated that the average cost of attending an adult education course in Ireland increased by about 30% between 1986 and 1987.(90) It comments:

> *Because of the high cost of the courses, the poor and generally disadvantaged members of our society are being excluded from adult education. They are the people with the greatest need, who would benefit most from participation. Most deplorable of all is the reduced access to literacy schemes throughout the country.*

Other barriers besides cost also exist: few adult education courses provide a crèche for instance, and if you are on social welfare only very limited further education options are possible. So adult education opens up opportunities for some people more than others. It especially disadvantages women and men from poorer backgrounds.

The social welfare system makes it very difficult for claimants to participate in education. If you are in education you are not considered to be 'available for work' and therefore unemployment payments are stopped. There is one very limited scheme, the Educational Opportunities Scheme, which allows claimants to study for an educational certificate, but it operates in only two areas of the country and in 1989 only fifty-seven people are benefiting from it. In any case, recipients of 'women's schemes' are not eligible.

HOUSING

Access to Housing Services
In Ireland owning your home is considered very important. With about 78% of homes owner-occupied, most people achieve that ambition - far more than in other European countries. Norway comes closest with about 67% of people owning their homes. A very high proportion of the Irish also own their homes outright, 47% of all households in 1987,

which means that they do not have a mortgage.(91) Many of these are helped to buy their homes by tax relief on mortgage interest and the substantial grants and subsidies to house buyers (in 1987 the government subsidy to owner-occupiers in tax reliefs and other measures was £218m, the subsidy to local authority tenants was £194m).(92) So the private home-owners benefit substantially from public money spent on housing: you have to be able to afford a mortgage to get the tax relief and the higher your rate of tax the greater the saving. *Property is one of the main forms in which wealth is held and created in Ireland, yet taxes on property are almost non-existent.*

Just over a fifth of Irish people do not have the opportunity or do not want to buy their own homes: they are either renting from local authorities or from private landlords (about 12% and 10% respectively of all dwellings in 1981). Far fewer women than men own their homes. Until recently, financial insititutions were reluctant to give a house purchase loan to a woman on her own. A mortgage is beyond the reach of the vast majority of low income people - the average income of those borrowing from building societies and banks in 1986 was £11,900, at that time the average payment to an unemployed household with two children was £4,095 a year. Women's incomes were even lower.

> *Despite the general rise in housing standards, certain groups have benefited little, or not at all, from the general improvement in housing conditions over the past decade or so. This is indicated by the stagnation, or even deterioration, in housing conditions which has occurred among those with the poorest quality of dwellings or with none at all. There has been an increasing disparity between the quality of housing services enjoyed by most households, and those obtained by those at the bottom end of the housing market.(93)*

Relying on local authority or private renting can lead to difficulties. In the private sector for instance, the tenant has few or no rights: rents are largely uncontrolled, there is no obligation to provide a rent book, one is entitled to a lease only after twenty years' continuous occupation, and frequently the accommodation is in poor condition. There is little official scrutiny of either the conditions or the charges for this rented accommodation. Nor do people renting privately get tax subsidies, although some get help with rent through the Supplementary Welfare Allowance (SWA). The use of this scheme for help with rent and mortgages has shot up since the beginning of the 1980s: nearly 9,000 people had to get this form of help from the SWA in 1987, whereas only about 1,300 received this help in 1980.(94)

The existence of public rent or mortgage subsidies has not eliminated local authority rent arrears - an average of 40% of tenants were in arrears among five local authorities in mid-1988.(95) You have to have a very low income to get SWA assistance with rent and people with mortgages only receive assistance with the interest part of the repayments. So the true number of people who have serious difficulty paying their rent or mortgage is unknown.

Women rearing children on their own have particular housing difficulties. Single parent households, which are only a tenth of all households, made up 20% of those on the local authority housing waiting lists in 1987. They are often forced to rent privately because they are a low priority for local authority housing which in Ireland has favoured large families and the elderly. When more public housing became available over the past few years, especially in Dublin, women on their own with children, single women and homeless women were housed in increasing numbers. However, they were generally moved into low demand areas. For example, over a third of 'homeless' people housed in one large suburb of Dublin in the last six months of 1986 were women parenting alone.(96) Problems in low demand areas include poor facilities in shopping, playgrounds and public services. Fewer shops means higher prices, while a lack of play areas keeps children around the home all day. Maintenance is another problem. With the cut-backs in spending to local authorities in recent years, maintenance budgets have been reduced. It is women who suffer most from ill-maintained housing because they spend more time than other family members in the home. And, of course, isolation is also a problem for women, especially those rearing children on their own, without central leisure facilities, adequate transport, and so on.

The conditions in which travellers live are very poor. Half of all travellers are without either piped water, a toilet or electricity.(97) The conditions in houses or chalets are usually better than this but a sizeable proportion of travellers on serviced sites are without piped water (22%) or a toilet (38%), while nearly all are without electricity. Roadside travellers have the worst living conditions: all but a tiny minority are deprived of all basic amenities. A recent report commented:

> *No amount of romanticism about the freedom of the open road can gainsay the vital fact that Irish Travelling people pay for their style of life and their low status in Irish society with levels of illness and deprivation long since thought intolerable in European society generally.(98)*

Poor services cause special hardship for traveller women.

There is very little emergency accommodation available for women who have to leave home because of violence. This is happening to a much greater extent nowadays and women are forming an increasing proportion of the homeless, along with young people. In 1988, 413 out of a total of 961 people living in hostels for the homeless in Dublin were women - most had left home because of violence. Most of the provision that exists is for men and a lot of the available accommodation (mostly hostels, many of them very old and in poor condition) is not suitable for the needs of women and children. In February 1988 hostels providing emergency accommodation in Dublin for women and children had an occupancy rate of 162%. In one hostel 16 women and children shared one room to cook, eat, sleep and spend their daytime hours.(99)

The full extent of homelessness among women is unknown but it is likely to grow among both women and men in the future as the house building programmes of local authorities come to a virtual standstill. Only an estimated 1,000 new local authority houses were completed in 1988 (compared with around 5,800 per year over the previous ten years) and only around 100 new houses were planned to be started in 1988. Put this alongside the fall that has occurred in private rented accommodation and the rise in waiting lists for public housing and another housing crisis looks to be looming.

LEGAL SERVICES

Access to the Law and Legal Services

The law is often thought of as 'out there', as an entity which does not touch everyday lives. And yet the law intervenes often, influencing especially relationships within the family. Marriage is, after all, a contract which is legally binding and carries with it economic and social obligations between partners and towards their children. This side of marriage tends to be overlooked, usually surfacing when a marriage breaks down. Then, the questions of custody, maintenance, ownership and division of property that arise show marriage at heart to be an economic and legal relationship.

Legal services are one of the most expensive services of all. Some of the top legal representatives charge more than £1,000 a day for their services. Following the European Court of Human Rights' ruling in 1979 that Josie Airey had a right to legal representation even though she could not pay for a private solicitor, the Government introduced a civil legal aid scheme. This scheme operates through twelve full-time law centres (six of which are in Dublin) and eighteen part-time centres. The service is inadequate to meet the need for legal aid. Some areas are totally without a service and some centres have to be regularly closed to the public to catch up with the backlog of work. The Legal Aid Board estimates that at least thirty-three full-time centres would be required to meet the demand. Apart from inadequate staff and resources, one type of law dominates: over 97% of the case work is family law. Areas not covered include social welfare and other appeals, consumer law, housing-related matters, criminal law. The legal aid services are not in fact free, all users have to make a contribution, the minimum charge being between £10 and £15 per client. Apart from the Legal Aid Board services, there is very little option for low income people: the Coolock Community Law Centre serves part of the north side of Dublin city and the Free Legal Advice Centres (FLAC) operate limited services on a voluntary basis in Dublin, Cork, Galway and Dundalk.

Far more women than men rely on the 'free' legal services. Of those who received advice and representation from the Legal Aid Board in 1986, 83% were women. Similarly, women are the major users of the Coolock Community Law Centre: of a sample of its cases over the last thirteen years, twice as many cases were brought by women. And yet there are women who cannot afford to get legal representation: 15% of a sample of women seeking maintenance orders from their husbands in the Dublin area had no legal representation in court (only 12% had a solicitor through the civil legal aid scheme).(100) Apart from money, people on low incomes may be distanced from legal services by factors such as their own lack of confidence, the complexity of legal language and the physical remoteness of legal services from their own communities.

So, the poor's access to the most vital public services, education, housing and the law, is not guaranteed and in many ways these services reinforce differences between people, especially women and men, rather than breaking them down.

SHE IS NOT AFRAID OF BURGLARS

Rita Ann Higgins

It's lunchtime
and he's training the dog again.
He says to the dog in a cross voice
"Stay there"
The dog obeys him.

When he goes home
he forgets to leave the cross voice
in the green where he trains the dog
and spits out unwoven troubles
that won't fit in his head.

He says to his wife,
"Stay there"
His wife obeys him.
She sees how good he is with the dog
and how the dog obeys his cross voice.

She boasts to the locals,
"I would never be afraid of burglars
with my husband in the house".

The locals, bursting for news, ask her,
"Why would you never be afraid of burglars
with your husband in the house?"

She calls a meeting at Eyre Square
for half three that Saturday.
Standing on a chair, wiping her hands
on her apron, she explains.

One day, she says, in a cross voice,
"the dog disobeyed my husband
and my husband beat him across the head
with a whip made from horse hair.

That is why I am not afraid of burglars
with my husband in the house"

First published in *Witch in the Bushes*. Galway,
Salmon Publishing, 1988.

6

POVERTY DAMAGES WOMEN'S HEALTH

From a health perspective rather than a medical one it is health institutions which are peripheral, and women, as mothers, carers, providers of food, organisers of safety, and negotiators are the ones who play the most central role.(101)

Health is a recurrent theme in women's conversations about poverty. Ill-health and poverty are seen to go hand in hand. Eating the same low-cost food eventually affects your health. A permanently inadequate diet, in some cases with bread, cornflakes and tea as staples, does not make for healthiness. Nor does living in poorly-maintained housing, often damp and overcrowded. Cutting back on food and fuel over a long period of time, combined with the stress of managing an inadequate income, sooner or later takes its toll on women's health. It is not easy to get women to talk about their own health - usually their first concern is for the health of their children, partners, parents, friends, and so on. Only with much probing will women talk about the effects of poverty on their own health. While health has become a major political issue with the recent spending cut-backs, women have been especially affected. Reducing public spending on health increases women's unpaid work because they are almost always the 'community carers'. Women living on low incomes are the most affected of all.

The gap in information is mirrored at an official level as well. The available statistics measure hospital treatment and mortality and morbidity rates mainly. Very little is still known about women's health. One review concluded:

We had expected to find in existence a large accepted body of knowledge and theory about the actual health status of women and the factors affecting it positively and negatively, a body of

*knowledge around which people could work away,
adding a bit here, changing a bit there, and
generally extending the terrain of the known.
Instead, the scene was more like a vast sea of
ignorance dotted with a number of isolated islands
of information around which hypotheses were built.
(102)*

While there is some information on what kills the Irish and
how hospitalisation is used, we have little sense of how well
people are and what are their health needs. Feeling out of
sorts, being dissatisfied or unhappy never gets to be a health
statistic. The medical profession's priorities are reflected in
the information made available by official sources and the
treatment received. Women from low income and other
backgrounds have been critical of this and other aspects of
health care.(103)

Women's Critique of Conventional Medicine
Control over their own health is of increasing concern to
women, with relationships with medicine and the medical
profession being especially criticised:

*... over the past one hundred and fifty years or so,
doctors on both sides of the Atlantic have
successfully 'medicalised' a number of human
phenomena ranging from madness to childbirth,
such that, supported by the law, doctors have now
almost a complete monopoly over the management
of these events.(104)*

Medicalisation has meant control by men because, as in
other areas, women are largely excluded from decision-
making in health: doctors and consultants and other authority
figures are predominantly men. Medicalisation has had two
very serious consequences for women:

* it has meant that reproductive health, and a particular view
  of it, has dominated, underemphasising other aspects of
  health and especially the health of older women

* women have been rendered powerless and dependent on a dominantly male medical profession.

Because we do not define our own healthiness, we may not always even recognise ill-health in ourselves. When women living on very low incomes are asked about their health, tiredness, fatigue and headaches are frequently mentioned. These are not illnesses so conventional medical treatment, the usual if not the only type available through the public health system, is inappropriate. We have been taught to judge our healthiness in medical terms, by such yardsticks as the number of visits to GPs, medicines, and so on. Similarly, many of the health problems experienced exclusively or mainly by women - such as period pains, cystitis, problems with contraception, post-natal depression - are either under-researched or not taken seriously by doctors. For example, over 60% of women are believed to suffer from one or more of the symptoms of Pre-Menstrual Syndrome (PMS) with 10% experiencing them as a problem (105), and yet so little is known about the condition that few women get relief. Health has also become compartmentalised - more often than not being divorced from the environment - so the symptoms rather than the cause may be dealt with. The ready prescription of tranquillisers is a particularly good example of this orientation. Many prescriptions are handed out each year to women suffering from the effects of poverty - poor housing, mental and physical ill-health, undernourishment, domestic violence. If poverty is the cause, then dealing with it is integral to improving healthiness.

Women's Approaches to Change
Women from different classes are increasingly active in trying to discover and reclaim their health. For example, the topic of health dominated the many meetings held by women in the lead-up to the National Tribunal on Women's Poverty on 30 September/1 October 1988. A seminar on health organised by the Council for the Status of Women in February 1988 attracted more than 500 women.

Three main approaches to change have been used by women in Ireland. The first is to set up self-help and development groups and activities to provide information and support to women around their health needs. Aspects of women's health hidden in conventional medicine are raised and discussed: sexuality, lesbian health and well-being, women and AIDS, assertiveness, the health effects of abortion and reproductive technologies.

A second approach has been to question the authority of the medical profession and its consequences for women. The paternalistic way that many doctors treat women has become an issue among women's groups. Assertive women in poor communities are particularly questioning doctors' readiness and capacity to understand their lives in poverty and therefore to comprehend the nature of their ill-health. Among the issues raised at the 1988 women's seminar on poverty was the failure of the medical profession to treat the underlying condition, rather than the symptoms.(106) The conventional doctor-patient relationship was also criticised. Many examples were given of doctors' insensitive and patriarchal treatment of women patients: using complex terminology without explanation, discussing a woman's condition with someone else (even her husband) without acknowledging her presence. One woman decided that she had had enough when the doctor insisted on addressing her and many other women patients as 'mammy'. Women's powerlessness, because of their lack of assertiveness, their lack of access to either another doctor or to alternative medicine was a central theme at this seminar. This theme was repeated at a subsequent workshop on women's health - along with the scarcity of comprehensive information about women's health and the social and economic factors that reduce women's health choices.(107) The potential of alternative medicines is also being explored by women, but because of high cost, and the difficulty of getting information about them, alternative forms of medicine are not often available to women living on low incomes.

The third general strategy for change has centred on a woman's right to reproductive control over her own body. Health has been the issue which has mobilised the largest numbers of Irish women during the last twenty years. At the beginning, access to contraception and services for women abused through sexual or other forms of violence, dominated. Very imaginative strategies (who will forget the contraceptive train to Belfast in May 1971?)(108) - were used to highlight women's lack of choice in health care and especially in relation to reproduction. Subsequently, women themselves became involved in health provision - services like the Rape Crisis Centres, the Family Planning Clinics and the Women's Aid Refuges being set up and run on a voluntary basis. Today, these services still rely significantly on voluntary labour and funding. The most recent activity around women's right to choose was centred on abortion. Up to 1983 and the time of the referendum on the eighth amendment to the Constitution (which gave the foetus full right to life), abortion was not a very public issue among women in Ireland. However, as well as being debated ardently at the time, women's right to choose has been an ongoing issue, and especially following the 1988 Hamilton judgement on the unconstitutionality of making information about abortion in other countries available to women in Ireland.

THE LINKS BETWEEN WOMEN'S POVERTY AND HEALTH

The available evidence from the Department of Health shows major improvements in the Irish population's health since the Second World War. Adult mortality rates have fallen considerably (from 12.3 in 1961 to 8.8 in 1987). The infant mortality rate in 1986 was 8.7 (per 1,000 live births), comparing well with most of our European neighbours and with its 1961 level of 30.5. Maternal mortality rates are also falling: 4 women died in childbirth in 1986 giving a maternal mortality rate of 6.5 (per 100,000 live births). People generally are living longer, healthier lives. However, the official statistics and other information, when available, also demonstrate that there is a relationship between women's poverty and ill-health. A recent review of health issues in Ireland says: *Women in the lower socio-economic groups are at a disadvantage in relation to health, both in employment and in home duties.(109)*

The main known health ill-effects experienced by women on low incomes, in comparison with other women, are as follows:

Women Living on Low Incomes

* Shorter life span
* Higher risk of depression
* More health hazards in the home and at work
* Higher risk of violence
* Greater risk of illness
* More likely to smoke
* Less informed about preventive health
* Less access to and choice of contraception
* More of their babies die as infants
* Larger numbers of children
* Less choice of health service.

1. Life Span and Physical Health

Life expectancy is a well-used measure of health - we can expect to live longer as improvements in medical technology, higher standards of living, and so on lengthen average life span. Women have always lived longer than men and continue to do so: women born in Ireland in 1982 could expect to live for five and a half years more than men - to 75.6 years as against 70.1 years for men. Irish women's greater life expectancy over men is small by international standards - women here have yet to reach the life span of our European neighbours, apart from the Portuguese.(110) Since life expectancy decreases with lowering income, women who are poor live shorter lives than more affluent women. *Travellers' life expectancy is little more than half that of the rest of the population.*

Living to old age has serious health and financial implications. As people age, they become more vulnerable to illness and disability. For instance, women are a majority (65%) of those in long stay geriatric units (over 9,000 women in 1985).(111) According to the *Census*, elderly women are also more likely to live alone, thereby increasing their risk of poverty. If one has lived on low income throughout one's life, hardship and poverty are more likely in old age. So, women who are now poor are unlikely to have any personal savings or other resources as they age which will reduce their options for care.

When women die, it is likely to be from heart disease,

87

cancers, strokes or breathing-related diseases. Women are more prone than men to strokes and other diseases of the blood vessels and they are also more likely to die from pneumonia and other breathing-related diseases. Cancers are an increasing cause of death here, for both women and men (although we still have fewer deaths from cancer than most of our European neighbours). Cancers killed over 20% of all the women who died in 1987, although women die from different cancers than men: breast cancer was the cause of a fifth of women's deaths from cancer in 1987 (killing 589 women) and cervical cancer killed a further 65 women. The highest risk cancer for women is cancer of the breast.(112) Stomach and lung cancer are the most widespread cancers among men. Irish women's health compares unfavourably with women from other European countries. Along with women from parts of Britain, Irish women have the highest death rate from heart disease of all the EC countries - men's death rates from heart disease are also very high - and we also have higher than average levels of lung cancer and cancer of the colon.

Although little information is available on how income group affects death rates, Irish patterns are likely to be much the same as those of other countries where less money means poorer health. The Black report, one of the most famous investigations of health, found very wide differences in health by social class in Britain in the late 1970s. 'Material deprivation' was the major source of health inequalities. Existing health services in Britain were said to be widening rather than narrowing the health divide.

What Makes Women Ill?
Marriage is the flippant answer - marriage seems to protect men from mental illness while increasing the risk for women. However, it is more complex than this. Women's occupations have to be taken into account first of all. Many employed women work in jobs with health hazards - think of Visual Display Units (VDUs) in office work, the chemical preparations used in hairdressing, laundry work, dry cleaning, and so on.(113) And much of women's work is very stressful - women clerical workers, for instance, have a high risk of coronary heart disease. Not only is very little known about the effects of work-place hazards but most areas where women

work are either not covered or are inadequately covered by protective legislation.

Women working in the home - a place not usually associated with health hazards - are particularly at risk.(114) Poverty damages relationships and women (along with their children) often bear the brunt of this. Male violence is one of the main health hazards in the home. *So home is not always a safe place*. While there are no definite figures on the extent of violence in the home, it seems to be quite widespread. In 1987, for instance, there were over 3,500 applications for barring orders to the courts (of which 44% were successful). A study of women in refuges found that over half had been beaten either on a daily or weekly basis (115), while other research on women in a poor community in Dublin found that 30% had experienced violence, with depression as one of the consequences.(116) Home becomes especially dangerous to health when it is in poor condition, exposing people, and women especially, to dampness and cold. Work in the home, along with many women's jobs, has many of the characteristics associated with stress: monotony and repetition, underutilisation of skills, low status, no monetary reward.(117) Add to this the very long hours worked and it is little wonder that depression is associated with full-time work in the home.

2. Mental Illness

> ... *the figures may be said to show more about psychiatry than they do about women.(118)*

Stress is a term that is increasingly used nowadays to describe the conditions under which many people live their lives. Women are increasingly pressurised - in employment, in school, in the home to compete for the highest standards of hygiene and cooking, in relationships to be more attractive, thinner, and so on. Pressure shows itself in different ways.

Women are especially vulnerable to depression, particularly when living on low incomes: 18% of women in one poor community in Dublin were estimated to be at risk of depression.(119) Poverty, housing difficulties and the fact that they have less control then men over their lives and relationships are all contributory factors to mental ill-health

89

among women living on low incomes. Added to this is the trauma of unemployment which is frequently thought of in relation to men only. Research says differently:women's mental health is significantly affected by their husband's work situation, his unemployment increasing her distress, even if she is herself employed.(120)

Women's mental ill-health is different in nature, being more hidden and more widespread, from that of men. It has long been the case that more Irish men than women are hospitalised for psychiatric illness. When illness is separated from institutionalisation, the main difference between men and women is the way their illnesses are dealt with or managed by the medical authorities. Men have more of the illnesses - schizophrenia, alcohol-related problems - for which people in Ireland are hospitalised. So, Irish men, especially those living in rural areas, have a higher rate of being diagnosed as schizophrenic and of becoming dependent on specialist psychiatric services.(121) Depression, on the other hand, which is far more common among women is less visible and does not attract the same amount of medical or other attention as an illness like schizophrenia. This means that women suffering from depression are less likely to be receiving any kind of treatment and are certainly less likely to be hospitalised.

> *Women go to doctors (usually General Practit-*
> *ioners) to relieve their psychological suffering*
> *because there is no other treatment alternative.*
> *They remain with the service because the General*
> *Practitioner does not have the ability to solve*
> *problems which are more social than medical in*
> *nature and origin and this problem continues even*
> *if they are referred to specialist psychiatric*
> *services.(122)*

So, many women do not appear in the official statistics or are persistent users of services which can only respond in a limited way to their needs. Health needs often go unmet as services based on a medical model are incapable of dealing with them.

Fewer women than men are admitted to psychiatric hospitals

for treatment each year. However, such figures are not a full statement about mental ill-health since many people are treated as out-patients - almost 30,000 in 1985 - or they may receive no treatment at all. Women are high users of outpatient services where they exist, although, because of gaps in service, many women especially in rural areas use their local doctor for problems of depression and anxiety.(123) More detailed information on all forms of psychiatric care confirms a much smaller gap between men and women than the official figures show: more women than men in Dublin were receiving psychiatric treatment in 1982 and double the number of women were receiving treatment for depression.(124)

Social class affects both the prevalence and treatment of all kinds of mental illness. The lower income groups have a greater chance of being diagnosed as mentally unwell and of being hospitalised for it: hospital admission rates in 1984 were six times greater for those from unskilled manual backgrounds than for employers and managers.(125) This gap, which is particularly high for schizophrenia and depression, is not decreasing.

For many years orthodox medicine has claimed, without strong evidence, that women's higher prevalence of depression and anxiety was due to a biological weakness, an inferiority, a genetic predisposition. Recent research contradicts this: when women and men in similar life circumstances in early adulthood are compared there is little or no difference between them.(126) As women's and men's lives develop and mature, women experience more mental distress and illness, particularly when working full-time in the home. The social conditions of low income women's lives - the fact that they work so hard and for such long hours, their increasing poverty, the conflicting roles which they often experience - have all added to their stress level. In this situation, all women, but especially those on lower incomes with young children, are at risk of depression and other forms of mental ill-health.

3. Greater Risk of Physical Illness
When poor, women's risk of illness is increased by many factors. With regard to preventive health care, for instance,

recent research by the EC found that 55% of Irish women over the age of 15 said that they had never had a cervical smear test.(127) The numbers having regular smear tests varied from a quarter of women with a low educational level to 43% of those with a high level of education. Smoking among women, now known to be associated with a wide range of illnesses, and especially heart disease and certain cancers, is highest among women in the lower socio-economic groups. Despite the risks, many women continue to smoke and many young women are taking up the habit each year. Recent figures show that almost as many women are now smoking as men (close to a third of each sex) and that smoking among younger, working-class women has been increasing consistently. Almost double the number of people in the lowest income brackets smoke (38%, as against 22% of the highest socio economic group).

Alcohol use and alcohol-related problems are also increasing among women. In the ten years to 1982, rates of alcoholism among men increased by 20%, according to Department of Health statistics, while the rates among women grew by 56%. In 1984, 1,342 women received treatment in a psychiatric hospital for alcohol-related problems. These statistics are not the whole picture because many alcohol-related problems are not treated in hospital. If trends here follow those elsewhere, alcohol-related problems are likely to grow among women, particularly given the ambivalence about alcohol in our culture. Alcohol-related problems have another side for women as well. Since so many Irish men are heavy drinkers and have alcohol-related problems, many women have to live with the problems that result, shortage of money, sometimes violence, loss of job.

There are other ways in which women's risk of illness increases. They experience a lot of pressure *not* to be ill - since women do most, if not all, of the work within the home, chaos is likely to result when a woman is in bed ill. Single parent families have no substitute for the mother or father. As well as this disincentive, women tend to put the welfare of other members of the family before their own. This again reduces their likelihood of receiving proper care when ill.

Information on preventive health is scarce among low income groups. Where nutrition is concerned for instance, people in the upper income brackets are far better informed about food values.(128) Although in most classes women are better informed, men's food preferences have a greater influence on the food that is purchased. Lower income groups also have less information on the dangers of smoking.

4. Birth Control and Family Planning

Control over their own fertility has always been held out as a vital condition of women's liberation. Progress on this in Ireland has been very slow, despite the fact that so much of women's effort and activity has been directed towards health. Even though women succeeded in providing much needed services largely through their own effort and unpaid or low paid labour, the state has not committed itself to providing essential services for women - £140,000 was spent by the Department of Health under the heading 'family planning' in 1986, out of a total health budget of £1.2 billion.

The use of medical contraceptives is very strictly controlled by legislation: only non-medical contraceptives, such as condoms, can be purchased freely in pharmacies (and this only since 1985). Women on low incomes have a very limited choice of contraception. No form of contraceptive is available as such to women with medical cards, although the Pill can be prescribed for other purposes. Launching its annual report for 1988, the Irish Family Planning Association (IFPA) said:

> *Women from lower socio-economic groups have to beg for medical services simply to exercise their right to choose the number of children they have. During 1988 alone, just under 12% of first time attenders at IFPA centres had not the financial means to exercise the right to control their own fertility. The IFPA are particularly concerned that many couples face unplanned pregnancies simply because they have no financial alternative.(129)*

So if women on low incomes want contraceptives and if their doctor is not prepared to break the law, they have to buy them, even at the Family Planning and Well Woman Clinics where a visit to the doctor is required for contraceptives. This situation prompted one local women's group to declare:

'No sex is safe sex'

Women who are poor frequently have difficulty getting information about different forms of contraception and associated health risks. As a result the developments in family planning seem to have passed some women in lower income groups by: one study found no increase in the uptake of family planning services by women from poorer backgrounds over the last five years.(130)

Contraceptive practices reflect the limited availability of services and also catholic church teaching on family planning. Over a quarter of 493 women surveyed in late 1985/early 1986 were using contraceptive methods with which they were not satisfied.(131) Natural methods were the most often used (by 35%), and also the most often regarded as unreliable. The pill was the next most common form of contraception (33%). While 84% did not wish to become pregnant, 7% of these were not actively avoiding pregnancy and abstinence was the only method used by a further 8%. Other research suggests that rural women make less use of contraception, relying on the natural, and more unreliable, methods.(132) This is hardly surprising given their distance from family planning services and the likelihood that contraceptives may not be supplied by the local pharmacy(ies).

Women's health options, especially their reproductive health and choices, are in many cases out of their hands: the medical profession and health administrators have the control. In Ireland, catholic values influence health service provision in a major way. The majority of hospitals, which receive most of their funding from the state, were founded and many continue to be run by religious orders. A catholic ethos prevails in these hospitals and Ethics Committees exist to ensure that these values are upheld. So, it is the Committee, rather than the individual physician and or the patient, which decides appropriate treatment in many cases, especially in relation to reproductive health. Many catholic hospitals will not perform sterilisations for example. And of course, this lack of means to control fertility is reflected in birth rates, which, while falling, are still high by international standards.

5. Women as Mothers

Irish women, by international standards, have high numbers of children: the birth rate was 16.6 per 1,000 of the population in 1987, compared with a French rate, the European country nearest to us, of 13.9 in 1985. Other European countries actually have a declining population. The birth rate here, although high, is falling however: in 1980 it was 21.8. The traveller community has an extremely high birth rate: the average traveller woman bears ten children. Although family size is falling there are still very many women rearing large families - 13% of mothers who gave birth in 1987 already had four or more children. There is a class difference again here: women from poorer backgrounds have more children.

The number of babies born outside marriage is increasing, reaching 10% of all births in 1987. Ten years earlier just 4% of all babies were born outside marriage. Many babies born outside marriage are born to women from lower socio-economic backgrounds: 55% of all non-marital births in 1983 were to mothers from semi-skilled and unskilled backgrounds.(133) While not all of these women will rear their children alone, a significant proportion of them will be lone mothers and therefore run a high risk of poverty since many are from low income backgrounds. Many are also very young: 30% (nearly 2,000) were aged 19 or less in 1987, according to Department of Health statistics, while 185 of single mothers were aged 16 years or less.

There are good grounds for concern about pre- and post-natal care. A Department of Health Survey in 1981 indicated that 23% of mothers did not visit a doctor before the 16th week of pregnancy and that some mothers did not attend regularly for ante-natal care.(134) Class differences emerged very clearly: the care of single mothers and those in the lowest income groups was particularly poor. Women from the traveller community also make much less use of health and GP services during pregnancy and their babies are lighter when born and have a higher than average risk of infant mortality. One of the main risk factors for maternal health - poor nutrition - is outside the control of the medical profession. The situation of women on low incomes is especially worrying since these women's nutrition is often inferior to that of other women.

Alongside these statistics must be placed the fact that large numbers of Irish women travel to Britain each year for abortions. The numbers taking this option have increased very rapidly over the last two decades: up to 4,000 women having abortions in Britain each year give an Irish address. This figure probably seriously undercounts the number of Irish women having abortions - particularly since Irish women may be less likely to give a home address following the eighth amendment to the Constitution and the Hamilton judgement. Contrary to popular belief, it is not teenagers but adult women, from mainly urban areas, who find themselves in this situation.(135) Many had not been using any form of contraception when they became pregnant.

UNTITLED

Heather Brett

On the brink - again.
That old, familiar
prickling in my toes
that signifies no solid land ahead
only the recognisable uncertainty
of thin air I've plummeted through before:

Evidence of my many escapades
are caught here,
snagged by unforeseeable circumstance:
In some places the strips of flesh
are not quite withered,
the bloodstains, not quite dry

But here I stand
poised on this overhang,
the sheer drop tantalising:
A kamikaze thought -
am I masochist or lemming?
Or do I pray that the glue on my
feathered wings will hold
and that this time, I will surely soar?

7

SOME ACTION FOR CHANGE IN THE 1980s

*Feminism for the 1990s must address itself and be
relevant to the needs and concerns of women of
different classes and social situations, resisting the
temptation to blur the edges, to sink our differences.
We have always known that we draw strength from
our unity, in the 1990s let us gain our inspiration
from our diversity.(136)*

Women generally have been active at many levels since the
re-emergence of the women's movement in Ireland in the
early 1970s. The issues raised by women during this time
have become so much a part of public debate in Ireland today
that we tend to take them for granted. Equal opportunities,
contraception, divorce, violence against women are all terms
now in common currency; although only since the 1970s.
Efforts over time to bring about change in the position of
women, and the politics surrounding them, are an important
part of the backdrop to women's action on poverty today.
Here we concentrate on describing activity among, with or for
women who are poor. The purpose is to try and evaluate the
potential of local activity for bringing about significant
change in the situation of women who are poor. An outline of
some efforts for change at national level is given as
background information; it is not intended to be a general
analysis of all women's activity over the last two decades or
of the relationships between different groups of feminists in
Ireland.

Women's Efforts for Change
It is hard to credit just how recently women's issues were
raised for the first time; an Ireland where they were taboo,
subjects for neither public nor private debate, is difficult to
imagine. Picture for a moment the kind of Ireland from which

the contemporary women's movement emerged: a very traditional, catholic society where, for instance, single mothers and women living apart from their husbands had no right to social welfare - they either had to get a job, emigrate or depend on help from their families or charity. Contraception was illegal; women were forced to leave their jobs in the civil service and other sectors when they married; men had a greater right to unemployment and other welfare payments. A subservient role for women was locked into social structures by state services which mirrored the teaching of the male-controlled catholic church. The 1960s and 1970s brought economic transformation: new government policies opened up our economy and society to the outside world. Social change followed economic change and traditional values, attitudes and structures came to be increasingly questioned and challenged. Issues about women's lives - their role, status, opportunities and financial position vis-à-vis men - were forced to centre stage by women activists. Feminist activity in other countries was a major influence on this re-awakening in Ireland.

Perhaps the start of the most recent wave of women's activity in Ireland was in 1968 when a number of women's organisations, including the Irish Housewives Association (IHA) and the Irish Countrywomen's Association (ICA), formed an ad hoc committee to investigate discrimination against women.(137) Following a request from this group, a Commission on the Status of Women was set up by the government in 1970. The Commission reported in 1972, making forty-nine recommendations. The Council for the Status of Women, an umbrella group now with sixty-eight affiliated women's organisations, was formed in 1973, one of its functions being to monitor the implementation of these recommendations.

What we now think of as the feminist movement had a somewhat different history. The Irish Women's Liberation Movement (IWLM) was founded in 1970 by a small group of mainly professional women, many of whom were journalists.(138) Early on, discussion and consciousness-raising dominated. The movement framed six demands in its manifesto in 1971:

* equal rights in law
* equal pay and the removal of the marriage bar
* justice for widows, single mothers and deserted wives
* equal educational opportunities
* the right to contraception
* one family, one house

As priorities identified for political activity, they were not all-embracing: abortion, divorce, and many health issues were not among the main demands made because they were seen as divisive. Nor was poverty a specific issue, although the demand for justice for widows, single mothers and deserted wives was of course relevant to some groups of women living in poverty. A more radical group, Irishwomen United (IWU) which emerged in 1974, sought, in addition to the above aims, the recognition of motherhood and parenthood as a social function, state funding for women's centres and the right to self-determined sexuality.

The lack of initial emphasis on poverty may have been due to the fact that only small numbers of women from low income backgrounds were active in early feminist activity. The dominant belief was that the rights of all women should be the focus because women were oppressed as a group. The National Question overshadowed much of what was happening in Ireland at the time and this also led to divisions within the women's movement. Taken as a whole, the interests that dominated within the women's movement in Ireland were those of the middle classes. Equality was mainly defined in terms of equality with middle or upper class men. This did not change significantly in the intervening years: working class and poor women have tended to pursue their concerns independently of women from middle class backgrounds, if at all. However, a number of individual women who were involved in the women's movement went on to work with the first European Programme to Combat Poverty (1975-1980), some working directly with women on low incomes.

Despite many initial flamboyant demonstrations and pickets, protests and hard work over the next fifteen years, progress on the original aims was slow. Most activity centred on equal pay, the recognition of single motherhood and a right to contraception. Emphasis soon shifted from the ideological to a concern with service provision and building networks of support for women. AIM (the pressure group for family law reform), Cherish (a pressure group for single mothers) and Women's Aid (for battered women) all date from this period. The first of the Rape Crisis Centres followed in 1977. Each of these services is still funded significantly by voluntary effort, operating on a shoestring; attempts to get a substantial state commitment to these health services for women have not been very fruitful.

Collectively, women have had significant achievements over the last twenty years. The demands that endured were among the most centralised or acceptable of the original demands: equality in the workplace, contraception, social welfare for one parent families and for unemployed women. Were it not for the efforts of women, lobbying through trade union and other channels of influence, these and other developments are unlikely to have occurred. The extent to which the lives of women on low incomes have significantly improved is far from certain, however. Class and gender forces ensure that general freedoms for women only very slowly affect life in poor communities.

THE SITUATION TODAY

Over the last number of years, the economic climate has changed in Ireland and, with it, attitudes about women. In 1986, for instance, 55% of people agreed that when there is high unemployment married women should be discouraged from working.(139) The economic conditions in which the original demands for women were framed no longer exist. In a climate of high unemployment, increasing emigration and poverty, progress on women's issues, many of which challenge the basic structures of society, especially the power of the catholic church as well as right-wing ideologies, is difficult to achieve.

Traditionally, women have always been important in organised activities, although usually in a back-up capacity. A customary back-up role meant that women were often slow to organise around their own interests. This is changing, however. Judged in terms of the numbers of groups, certain activities among women appear to be flourishing. In particular, there has been a big growth in local women's educational and development activities in disadvantaged areas over the last four to five years. Women's groups come and go, products of a very insecure funding environment, but as far as we can ascertain a total of 166 women's groups or organisations are active now(140):

National Groups Campaigning on Women's Issues	21
Groups Providing Services for Women	21
Women's Special Interest Groups	18
Women's Studies Groups	8
Local Women's Educational and Community Groups	98
Total	166

Not all of these have a connection with poverty among women.

1. National Campaigning Groups

There are many different types of group involved here, ranging from the relatively long-established Council for the Status of Women to the very young Separated Women's Action Group. Some represent women in particular situations (such as widows, separated women), campaigning mainly for their members, while others campaign for an improvement in the position of all women. As far as we know, only two of the twenty-one campaigning groups were set up by women from low income backgrounds - Women Together Against Poverty and National Travelling Women's Forum. These are also among the most recent groups. The remainder are mainly professional women's groups, representing their members' interests, or are branches of other organisations, such as political parties. Only a handful are actively concerned with women's poverty and generally these groups are not representative of women from poorer backgrounds.

One of the groups most relevant to women living on low incomes is Women Together Against Poverty. Just under two years old, this group comprises traveller and settled working class women, mainly from the Dublin area. During 1988 they held a number of seminars and meetings on women's poverty.(141) Organised by and for women who are themselves poor, the purpose of the meetings was to enable women to discuss their own and others' poverty and to develop a plan of action. Seminars and meetings have been imaginative: drama, exercises and singing can be an integral part of meetings. Traveller women have also held a number of meetings themselves in 1989 with the support of the Dublin Travellers Education and Development Group.

2. Groups Providing Services and Support for Women
In the absence of state-provided services, groups were set up or found themselves involved in providing services for women. We know of twenty-one groups, most providing health-related services. They include the Rape Crisis Centres, Cherish, the Well Woman Centres and Women's Aid. Many combine service provision with active campaigning on relevant issues, like Focus Point which represents homeless women. These services, and others in, for example, publishing, education and so on, are a very concrete measure of women's achievement over the last twenty years. By and large they cross class boundaries, although since they have little guaranteed funding they have to charge for their services which may distance some women who are poor.

3. Women's Special Interest Groups
There are at least eighteen special interest groups. They are mainly professional groups which provide a point of contact for women with similar interests or those in the same job or profession. They are almost exclusively middle class. Included here are organisations such as the National Federation of Business and Professional Women's Clubs, Network (for women in business and management) and Irish Federation of University Women. Sometimes they are branches of international organisations. They do not usually become involved in political issues and they have no known links with women's activities at local level in poor communities, except in a charitable role.

4. Women's Studies Groups
There are a number of women's studies groups, active mainly

in the third-level education sector, holding lectures, seminars and publishing material on women. For the first time in Ireland, a graduate diploma in women's studies will be available in 1989 (from the University of Limerick) and post-graduate Masters Degrees in Women's Studies are planned for 1990 by Trinity College and University College Dublin. Women's studies courses are frequently available in arts and social science undergraduate degree programmes. UCD Women's Studies Forum is the longest established group: active since 1983, it is mainly involved in running fortnightly research seminars, lunchtime discussions, thematic conferences and in publishing reports of seminars. At a national level, most women's studies groups are linked into the Women's Studies Association. The fact that the Third International Interdisciplinary Congress on Women in Dublin in July 1987 was attended by over 600 Irish women (along with another 600 women from other countries) indicates a healthy interest in women's issues. A good deal of research on women is also underway.(142)

5. Local Women's Educational Groups/Projects
Women who are poor today are most active at local community level. There are at least ninety-eight local women's groups.(143) The majority of these are based in low income areas, being especially popular in Dublin: almost half of all groups are based in Dublin and most of the remainder are in the large provincial centres. Six counties had no known women's group in June, 1989 and most counties, apart from those with a large urban centre, had no more than one or two groups.(144)

These local women's groups are not easily categorised: some are educational or action projects, others are groups gathered together for a specific purpose, and still others have evolved from family resource centres or other activities. They are usually a response to poverty at local level, often initiated by a professional worker or developing out of another, typically a family-related, activity. Most of the local groups are relatively young (less than three years old); two Dublin groups - KLEAR (Kilbarrack Local Education for Adult Renewal) and CAL (Coolock Adult Learning) - are among the longest established, dating from 1982. Groups are, for the

103

most part, informally structured and self-directed. The demand can often be huge: the Coolock group had a 600% increase in attendance in four years. Other evidence of high demand also exists: local women's projects accounted for nearly a quarter of the 220 grant applications received by the Combat Poverty Agency in 1987.

Not always based on a worked-out philosophy, the groups usually aim to impart information and skills, while at the same time providing an environment where particpants can learn about themselves and develop a positive self-image. Self-development and group development are key objectives (see diagram). The educational content generally falls into four main areas: personal development and health; skills usually relating to domestic activities; academic subjects; information and discussion. Many of the groups encourage women to write about their experiences.

Being involved in these programmes has obvious benefits. Women on one course in Dublin, for instance, found that they were more confident as a result - separating their own identity from the way they were defined by others:

> *Personal development I found a bit heavy at first but after a few weeks I realised I hadn't really thought about myself as an individual, but after a few classes I began to get more dependent on myself, and I am more involved in things I thought I hadn't got the go for.(145)*

In the view of the participants, certain things enhance programmes: high involvement of participants in decisions about the programme; courses that are relevant to personal and family interests; participative learning sessions and creative methods; a crèche and a time schedule that accommodates people's family responsibilities.(146) A slogan of the KLEAR group is: 'No crèche, no class'.

Some Problems Affecting Women's Activity

Clearly, local level activity among women has great potential for change, although of course it also has to be accompanied by change at other levels. Considering women's activism generally, there are a number of difficulties at the present time, three of which stand out:

* little or no funding is available for activity among women at local level in poor communities
* related to this, women have not been sufficiently involved in politicisation work
* groups do not link with or network each other sufficiently

Limited Funding and Resources

There is no central source of funding for activity among women, especially for women in poor communities. The Combat Poverty Agency has made women's groups a priority for funding and the vocational education committees fund some educational work among women's groups. But funding from each of these sources is limited and the demand is huge. Nor is there any designated funding from the Arts Council for local women's arts or writing groups or indeed for any local writing groups. The number of programmes that fail to get underway or to survive because of the scarcity of available funding and resources is unknown. Most groups operate with minimal funding; when they do get funding it is mainly from state and semi-state sources, there are conditions attaching to it and it is for one year only.

Operating on a shoestring has many consequences: groups are limited in their learning content (they may be unable to pay tutors for instance); many have to rely on voluntary labour; they may be unable to afford a crèche (an essential for a women's group); and their time and energy can be absorbed by fund-raising. Most have access to local premises, usually from the vocational education committee, sometimes from the local authority. The premises are often in poor condition, however, and they are frequently shared with other groups. Some groups have a very short life span: depending on the energies of one individual or on insecure funding, they fail to survive.

The search for funding requires enormous energy and considerable skill. Given this and the fact that information about possible sources of funding is not freely available from a central source, to set up a group requires people 'in the know' or those who have influence. This may work against

Benefits of Local Educational Projects
According to Participants

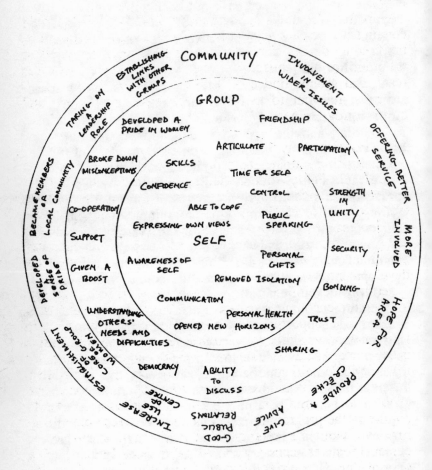

From: Women Learning.

initiatives by women who are themselves poor because they have difficulty getting the necessary information and resources to start up a group. Alternatively, it may force local groups to align themselves with individuals and organisations whose interests and political perspective may differ from theirs.

Apart from the limits on the scale of funding available, only certain activities are popular with funding agencies. In effect, the funding climate forces groups to tailor their activities to the priorities and concerns of the funding agencies with the result that groups find it difficult to pursue activities which are most relevant to them or to develop imaginative and creative programmes.

Little Politicisation

The funding climate more or less determines activities at local level. Fairly routine educational activities are most likely to be funded, hence the concentration on this type of work at local level. The short-term nature of most funding discourages the development of long-term programmes, at the same time increasing insecurity. In addition, participants can be limited to a single course each - a barrier to long-term developmental work and group work.

Personal development is the main focus of local activity. Women are encouraged to talk about their situation and their feelings in a supportive atmosphere and, at the same time, to learn or improve skills they may need as mothers and workers in the home. These activities can have an enormous impact on the individual participants: confidence grows, one develops a different perspective on one's own situation, and women are enabled to become part of a group, the friendships usually outlasting the programme or course. The courses help also to improve women's relationships with their children. A personal focus is necessary and desirable from the start, being one of the first principles of feminism. But, if an individualised focus continues, the programmes, while valuable for the participants in the short-term, will not lead to the types of collective orientation and activity which are necessary to bring about change in the position of women in poor communities. What many personal development courses do is to help women cope better with their immediate situation.

However, if only this focus persists, programmes are unlikely to lead to any long-term structural change, either in the position of the participants or of the many women who share the same situation.

> *Programmes to help find ways to deal with daily difficulties are not bad in themselves, but they are not neutral. They either help or hinder the struggle towards consciousness about the reasons for women's poverty.(147)*

Of course, lack of politicisation is not confined to women who are poor. But it is especially vital for women from low income backgrounds to become involved in these kinds of activities if they are to be active in changing their situation. What is needed is a *properly funded programme of development work among women in poor communities*. Based on an analysis of individual situations and how they link into the shared experience of all women in poor communities, the programme could develop a strategy for collective action, as well as individual change. The starting point could be the individual participants' own situation and the practical realities of their lives. Questions like the following need to be answered: Why is it that women's skills are so undervalued and most of women's work unpaid? Who has power over me as an individual and over us as a group of women? Where are the decisions that most affect our lives made and by whom? Leadership training is also vital. This kind of work is already being done by some projects, but it is insufficiently funded and under-resourced.

The activities of the Parents Alone Resource Centre in Coolock Dublin provide a model of the kind of developmental work that can benefit women who are poor. The Centre, which is one of nine local projects in Ireland being funded under the second European Programme to Combat Poverty, provides a comprehensive support and development programme for women lone parents. A primary aim, along with providing services, is to develop a core group of women lone parents and to give them relevant organisational and other skills as well as a political analysis of the situation of lone parents and other groups of women living in poverty in Ireland.

Ideally, a properly-funded and structured development programme with women should lead to:

* a sense of self esteem, self-worth, confidence and assertiveness
* knowledge of and a perspective on personal, local and national power structures
* a readiness to organise at local level and to become involved in existing local power structures as a start
* networking with groups and women in other low income communities to begin with, and in the long term, if desired, with women and men from other class backgrounds

Lack of Links or Networking

At a macro level, there is very little or no networking, either among local groups in different areas or between them and activity at national level. Like other community activities, they have no channel to link them to groups involved in similar activities in other areas or to national power structures. Because funding is largely uncoordinated and quite strictly controlled by funders, groups are often uninformed about what other projects are doing or they are in competition with one another. These factors are barriers to networking.

At a more general level, women's activity in Ireland has been divided by ideological differences: moral, political, class and sexual. Family-centred demands had the widest support from the outset but women continue to be divided on the more radical issues such as contraception, abortion, sexuality and on the national question. A broad-based political movement, founded on a clear feminist critique and policy and linking women across classes, never emerged in Ireland, or in other western countries. Instead, we had a series of more focused, single issue campaigns, such as the defend the clinics group, women's right to choose, the strip searching campaign. Where women came together on these single issue campaigns, a lot was achieved. However, today, the women's movement is fragmented.

Women from low income backgrounds have been largely outside the organised women's movement or, when they did become involved, their needs were largely unheard. If women living on low incomes want to work for change effectively they have had to set up their own organisations or groups to do so. Few issues around which women have organised over the past twenty years have crossed class boundaries organisationally, except perhaps the Campaign for a Unified Social Welfare Code, the Equal Pay campaign in the early stages, the campaign around the social welfare equality legislation in 1985/86, and issues related to violence against women to a lesser extent. Women in poor communities are hampered by their lack of resources and the class politics of the women's movement as a whole. Looking to the future, however, it is difficult to see how women from these communities can make significant progress on the issues that affect their lives in isolation from broader alliances. Whether these alliances are to be with organisations or women from other classes is one of the most difficult questions to be answered.

Recent history clearly suggests that any alliances between women from poor communities and other interests have to be selective ones. Rather than looking for a blueprint for change, to improve the situation of women who are poor will require many strategies and alliances. Before getting involved in any alliances, however, women living on low incomes must be very clear about their own needs and very assertive in voicing them. The concept of *control* is crucial: apart from one or two exceptions, women living on low incomes have not had a high degree of control in the alliances in which they have been involved up to now. Properly-funded politicisation work which recognises where power lies and how it is used - with women living on low incomes is a vital first step to any long-term change. Ideally, this must precede decisions about alliances, so that any coalitions between women living in poverty and other interests are founded on an understanding of the possible benefits and limitations of such alliances, and start from the interests and needs of women who are experiencing poverty.

WHO AM I?

Carmel McCarthy

I thought it would be easy to answer the question, 'Who am I?', but I am so many people everyday that sometimes I don't know who I am myself!

If the kids are sick, I am their nurse
When they're hungry, I am their cook
When the house needs cleaning, I am the maid
When the windows need cleaning, I am the window cleaner.

I am also a launderette operator, a messenger, a child-minder and accountant and a teacher.

I am a preacher when religion comes to mind, I'm also a referee when the kids start to fight.

(You are also a sex slave to your husband whether you know it or not)

I'm also a person who makes decisions, big or small, but always hoping for the best.

When you take your marriage vows, the priest says 'for better or for worse' but never tells you how many people you are expected to be. So you don't know until you sit down and think about it, then you realise who you are.

You can't get sick because in the kids' eyes, mammies don't get sick, so you're meant to be strong. So I think you're an actor as well by pretending to be well when you're not.

Some women don't know that they are all these people, so now you can say that a woman works twenty-four hours day and night.

8

FIGHTING AGAINST WOMEN'S POVERTY

The struggle against poverty is a struggle of immense proportions. It is a struggle not just to achieve a fairer distribution of income and wealth, but to abolish distinctions of income and wealth themselves. It is a struggle to transform the basis on which society is organised: to replace a system based on the priority of profit and gain by one in which all can benefit from, just as all who are able can contribute to, the wealth and resources that human labour is capable of producing.(148)

Overview of Women's Poverty

A number of things are striking about women's poverty. As we have seen, it is very hidden and little is known about it. Going on national figures, a minimum of 274,000 women (compared with 244,000 men) are living on inadequate incomes, ie less than £48 a week for one adult. However, poverty lines are deceptive because they are usually based on household income and take no account of how money is shared out between members. So, it is possible that women are poor in households which in a survey would be above the poverty line because not enough money is passed on to them. The number of women in this situation, although unknown, is in addition to the above figure of the numbers of women in poverty.

Of course not all women are poor. Poverty is selective. Women with the highest risk of poverty include those rearing children on their own (of whom there are at least 80,000), some women based full-time in the home, especially those caring for an elderly relative, elderly women living alone, women in low paying jobs, traveller women and those who find themselves homeless. The sources of women's poverty are different to those of men. One of the key features of women's poverty is financial dependence - for many their income is out of their hands - two-thirds of Irish women depend on either a man or the state for their income. This reduces their access to and control over money. Over 60% of men in Ireland earn an income through paid work, compared with less than a third of women. Men's poverty is due mainly to unemployment and a high number of dependants. The assumption of women's dependency, or, to put it another way, that men will take care of women, has also justified low and no wages for women's work.

The accuracy of research on poverty and especially on women's poverty in Ireland and elsewhere cannot be taken for granted. In truth, it has been quite limited, confining its view of poverty largely to the economic and measuring it on the basis of family or houshold income. There are a number of points to be kept in mind when considering the results of research into poverty:

* the numbers of women in poverty are undercounted by most research
* signficant aspects of women's poverty have been ignored or under-emphasised
* there are no accurate fixed or objective measures of poverty
* social welfare rates are not based on the amounts people need to stay out of poverty
* poverty has generally been measured in a limited way, mainly in terms of money coming into the household or family

Perceptions of Poverty
Exploring poverty among women forces us to question conventional views of poverty: that it is mainly about money for instance. It is widely assumed that poverty can be understood in terms of financial shortages, bad budgeting, debts, and so on. Poverty is about much more than money. Personally, it means feeling inferior to other people, feeling inadequate in some way. Socially, it can mean isolation and living in a community where every one is in a similarly poor situation. At a cultural level, poverty distances people from creative ways of expressing themselves, through writing, art, drama or even music, and makes much of conventional and establishment culture foreign to them. Politically, poverty

113

means being removed from decision making, not having access either to power or to the people who make the decisions.

> *In the last analysis to be poor is not just to be located at the tail end of some distribution of income but to be placed in a particular relationship of inferiority to the wider society. Poverty involves a particular sort of powerlessness, an inability to control the circumstances of one's life in the face of more powerful groups in society.(149)*

Another misconception is that poverty can be understood in terms of people's situation at one point in time only. In fact to understand why some people are poor, we must consider their situation over time, even from generation to generation. Lack of access to resources, such as money or capital, education, housing, good health, and opportunities over the course of their lives separate the poor from the rest of the population. People do not just wake up poor one day. The challenge is to try and understand the experiences that people who are poor go through and to identify the processes that select some for poverty, the majority for adequate income and still others for affluence and wealth. Two main factors shaping that process are gender and class position - gender keeps women as a group poorer than men and class keeps some people poorer than others. They are the key to understanding how and why one person is poor and another is not.

A FRAMEWORK FOR CHANGE

The measures that are needed for change depend on how the causes and effects of poverty are understood. Throughout this book, it has been emphasised that inequalities and poverty are based on both class and gender differences. So to eliminate poverty, direct intervention is needed to break down class and gender segregation. This means, among other things, that poverty among women will not be eliminated without measures to address poverty generally. But, because some aspects of women's poverty are due to the fact that they are women, actions to improve the position of *all* women are also integral to tackling women's poverty. But the experience of the past twenty years gives a very clear message: women who are poor are usually the last to benefit from sex equality measures. *Women on low incomes must be given priority if their situation is to be improved.*

Three sets of actions are needed:

* general measures to address poverty
* measures to improve the position of all women
* specific measures for women who are poor

The first links into the economic structure of society - how resources and rewards are distributed. The second concerns the continuing divisions and inequalities between women and men in our society; the third recognises that some women are doubly disadvantaged: by sex and by social class and that, without specific measures targeted to them, women who are poor will not benefit.

Measures to Combat Poverty Generally
Looked at in one way, the Irish economy seems to have done well over the last couple of years: profits are up, exports are high, there is a trade surplus and interest rates are stable. Economists agree that the economy performed well between 1987 and mid-1989. The upturn in the economy has not benefited everyone. There is no evidence to support the notion that a rising tide floats all boats. If we consider Ireland's experience over the 1960s and 1970s, we find that growth did not break down inequalities and, in some cases, even worsened them.(150)
Alongside the selective growth there is:

* a very high national debt (in the region of £25 billion owed to Irish financial interests and foreign bankers)
* a huge outflow of profits from this country each year, undertaxed (estimated at £1.6 billion in 1988)
* high emigration (estimated to be between 30,000 and 45,000 in 1989)
* high unemployment (235,00 approximately in 1989)
* very high poverty (up to a third of the population)

Ireland's economic dependence on international capitalism explains why some of these problems persist. A key aspect of our development strategy over the last thirty years was to encourage foreign trade and to get multi-national companies to locate in Ireland. As a consequence, we became dependent on multi-nationals - they now own 55% of our industrial assets - and remain so, even though they are leaving the country in the search for even greater profits. Our policies, especially taxation policies, are biased in favour of large industrial and business interests. When cuts in expenditure have been made, it is public services that have been affected, services vital to the poor - health, education, social welfare and housing. When tax cuts have been made, they have mainly benefited the better off, leaving the structure of the tax system unchanged and profits, especially, undertaxed.

To deal with poverty and the problems associated with it, state policies in taxation, education, housing and so on need to be far more redistributive. At present, state policies do not sufficiently prevent the cycle of privilege repeating itself, and in some cases they encourage and further it. The children of the better off gain most from the public money allocated to education every year. And yet, the better off are not dependent on public services, unlike the poor who cannot afford to buy essential services, such as health, education and housing, on the private market.

> *Eradicating poverty means redistributing resources and opportunities and changing the structures that exist at present.*

Change must happen at a number of levels:

* the social welfare system
* the taxation system
* public services
* the wages paid for work

None of these will be sufficient on their own. Unless a co-ordinated programme of action is taken by the state, there will be little change in the numbers of people in poverty.

Social welfare payments are too low and the rates have never been properly worked out. As a result, long-term poverty is not averted, both because of inadequate social welfare rates and because claimants get little positive encouragement and help to enter the jobs market. Also, women as a group receive less than men because many are treated as men's dependants. Among the most urgent changes needed are an increase in rates to the level recommended by the Commission on Social Welfare (£55 - £65 a week for an individual); this should involve disaggregation of payments so that each person gets a payment of their own; better provision for children; and an improvement in the way the system treats people. As a society failing to provide enough employment for people, we need to address poverty and in the meantime adopt the principle of social welfare as a right of all citizens.

Other state policies too reflect the interests and power of particular groups. In taxation, the PAYE sector is overtaxed while corporate or big business and agricultural profits, property and other ways of making money are under-taxed. The fact that wealth is virtually untaxed means that the state allows the wealthy to pass on their privilege to their children without interference. Public services such as health, education, and housing, should be directed more towards those on low incomes and, following the cut-backs of recent years, the quality of the services needs to be improved. Local services are particularly important for people living on low incomes for whom transport and access can be problems. Some action is also necessary on low wages and part-time work. *A statutory minimum wage would significantly improve income levels since at least a tenth of the poor are in low paying jobs.*

Job creation is a vital element in eliminating poverty and in stemming the growing tide of emigration. There must be funding for community development so that the effects of poverty at local level can be combated. Through a properly funded programme of community development, people in low income areas could build up structures with a strong local representation that can influence both local and national decisions in relation to resource allocation.

These and other changes will not come about of their own accord, in fact they are likely to be strongly resisted because they go against the interests of the powerful. The economic and social system currently divides rather than unites people. Unless people who are poor are widely supported and their demands endorsed by other sectors of the population, they will not get what they need and should have by right. People must lobby politicians and give their support to groups of social welfare claimants and others who are arguing for fundamental change.

Improving the Position of Women
There are a number of elements to this.

1. Women's Situation before the Law
Challenging the Constitutionality of different practices has been one of the main ways of changing the law. The most significant legal changes over the last two decades include the Family Home Protection Act in 1976 which ensured that the family home could not be sold by one spouse without the agreement of the other; since 1976 also spouses are legally obliged to support their partner and children; in 1981 barring orders were introduced; and since 1986 women are permitted to have their own, rather than their husband's, domicile.

But overall, legislation on its own has only a limited effect in bringing about change. In any case, progress in legal reform has been both slow and piecemeal - not least because it involves challenging the traditional legal and catholic values which are enshrined in the Constitution. The definition of rape remains very limited and measures to deal with violence in the home are inadequate. Significant legal barriers remain, not least in the Constitution:

> *A constitution which recognises that 'by her life within the home, woman gives to the state a support without which the common good cannot be achieved,' and which both prohibits divorce and equates the right to life of the mother with the right to life of the unborn child sets defined limits on the role of women in that society. (151)*

2. Women's Employment Situation
At first glance this is an area of great achievement: the marriage bar for women in jobs was removed in 1973; following membership of the EC, the Anti-Discrimination

(Pay) Act of 1974 and the Employment Equality Act of 1977 were introduced. These were the result of a campaign which continues to the present day. Pressure and vigilance from campaigning groups and organisations was needed to force employers to comply with the legislation, even the government itself tried to avoid equal pay in the public service in 1976! A fundamental difficulty with our legislation is that to qualify a woman must establish comparability with a male worker - difficult to do when so many women and men work at different types of jobs. The legislation has had a limited effect - in 1987 women's weekly wages in manufacturing were still no more than 60% of men's. Legislation is limited because it cannot get to the root of inequality and attack a sex segregation process that begins far earlier than when people take up employment. So, even if equal pay was fully implemented, women's earnings would probably rise no higher than 74% of men's.(152)

Very significant barriers still prevent women with children from working outside the home. Child care provision is at best patchy with no statutory service - workplace crèches exist only at the discretion of the employer, and can be very costly. Work is still organised very inflexibly in terms of male life-styles and life-cycles. Even if they are introduced, some flexible arrangements in jobs may work against the long-term career interests of women. Whether these are a cause or symptom of the problem is difficult to say. Some would say that barriers reflect a fundamental belief that married women with young children should not work outside the home if they do not need the money - a belief held by 58% of the population.(153)

Finally, there is the issue of family responsibilities: women cannot take an equal part in the labour market and in other areas of social and political life, unless men do an equal share of the work in the home. This has not happened. 80% of Irish women feel that they do most or all of the housework themselves.(154) Many women are doing two jobs: working full or part-time outside the home and doing most of the home-related work as well.

3. Women's Control Over Their Own Fertility
Family size is closely related to poverty - large families have

a very high risk of poverty. Yet although there have been improvements, many women who are poor lack the means to control their own fertility because the pill is the only contraceptive available on the medical card and they cannot afford to visit private clinics.

Irish women's right to contraception was hard won. Following a test case brought by Mary McGee in 1973, married women's constitutional right to import contraceptives for their personal use was asserted. In response to this, very limited legislation was introduced and it was not until 1985 that the sale of condoms without prescription to anyone aged 18 years and over was legalised.

Generally, Irish women still lack both the right of and access to a choice of free and safe contraception. Family planning services exist only on a limited and voluntary basis. Abortion is a criminal offence, and since a new amendment was added to the Constitution in 1983 the foetus now has an equal right to life to that of the mother. And the long trek of Irish women abroad for abortions continues.

4. The Situation of Women Within and Outside Marriage

To begin with the positive, most women rearing families outside of marriage are now entitled to social welfare. However, strict conditions attach to these and other 'women's schemes' which creates hardship for many women. Yet public maintenance is far better than private maintenance because it guarantees an income: only 9% of a sample of 1,127 maintenance orders made through the courts over the last ten years were operating satisfactorily.(155)

In 1986 a referendum to remove the Constitutional prohibition on the dissolution of marriage was defeated. So the Irish Constitution still prohibits divorce. Yet the catholic church recognises and will perform second marriages for people whose first marriage it has annulled. But civil annulment is very limited and very costly. In addition, many people are prevented from legalising their relationships. A judicial separation bill has just been passed, having taken two years to come through the houses of the Oireachtas, while a limited state-funded family mediation service exists since 1988, but only in the Dublin.

In general, the state's position on marriage is inconsistent.

Marital breakdown is considered an insurable risk for social insurance purposes (so 'deserted wife's', and from late 1989 'deserted husband's', payments exist). Marital property rights here are individualised while, for maintenance and taxation purposes, marriage is defined as a community of interests.(156) In turn the social welfare system treats women as dependent spouses.

Many concrete proposals for change have been made by groups and organisations including the Oireactas Joint Committee on Women's Rights and the Law Reform Commission - yet action is very slow. In the absence of far-reaching legislative change, marital breakdown continues without remedy: in the 1986 *Census* 37,000 people said they were separated, 60% of them women. The majority were separated without a legal sanction or deserted. Other evidence confirms marital breakdown as a growing problem: 6,000 people sought advice on judicial separation from the Legal Aid Board in 1986, double the number the previous year, and there was a 25% increase in the numbers seeking separation agreements. Apart from the failure to institute a variety of ways of dealing with marital breakdown, other problems exist for women: for instance, rape is still very narrowly defined here and rape within marriage is still not a legal offence. In addition, women still lack rights of ownership of the family home or other property and no account is taken of the contribution of the non-earning partner. So, women giving up work to rear children are in a very vulnerable situation should their marriage break down.

5. Equality in Relation to Social Welfare

In 1979 the EC passed an equality directive which ruled that women and men were to be treated equally in employment-related social welfare payments. It was 1986 before the changes were actually implemented in Ireland. The choice faced by the government was either to equalise upwards (to pay all claimants an adult dependant allowance for their spouses regardless of whether they had an income of their own) or to equalise downwards (to abolish payments for the spouse where she/he had an independent income). Equalising down was the option chosen. A positive outcome of the Directive was that married women could claim for dependants and got equal entitlement to unemployment benefits on the same basis as men and single women. While many families gained, at least 17,000 families lost some income. Following a lot of pressure from a coalition of women's and other interests, temporary 'cushioning' payments of either £10 or £20 a week were introduced to ease these families' transition to equality. These have been continued on an ad hoc basis but have not been increased in value since they were introduced.

While the Directive removed the grosser forms of discrimination, it has been described as 'piecemeal and cosmetic'.(157) Indirect discrimination was largely ignored which means that discriminatory questioning of women (about their domestic and childcare arrangements) was not outlawed. Also, the threshold of maximum earnings of £50 in the absence of a statutory minimum wage could be an incentive to employers to keep women's wages low and discourage women to take up a job outside the home. The Directive has led to no less than seven different proceedings before the High Court and many aspects of social welfare have been said to still directly and indirectly discriminate on the grounds of sex.(158)

The task of bringing about change is not helped by the current climate in which women's rights are regarded by many as a luxury. Over the last four or five years, women have had to expend a lot of energy defending legal and income maintenance rights already gained. *Clearly, a renewed and intensive programme of action is needed*. This should involve both legislative change and positive action programmes which recognise that women's disadvantage is built into structures. Until now a very narrow concept of equality has been used: somewhere between equality of opportunity and equality of participation. By and large, equality has been assumed to exist once the legal obstacles facing a woman as compared with a man are removed. This is not enough. Women are unequal across different areas of their lives - education, health, social welfare and work - and programmes designed for one or even two areas will not bring about sufficient change. *Values and ideology must also change*.

While the equality legislation must be monitored and rigidly enforced, on its own it has a limited impact. This was recognised from the start in the United States of America where equality legislation was accompanied by positive or affirmative action programmes. These programmes aim to undo the effects of past discrimination by changing attitudes and encouraging women to get involved in jobs and activities that are traditionally men's. Women must be encouraged and enabled to seek power - in politics, in business, in trade unions, and so on. Unless women are represented in fairly large numbers in the positions of power, they cannot influence change. But if women are to do this, certain basic facilities are needed, such as reasonably priced or free crèche and child minding facilities, especially for women on low incomes.

Even if sex differences are addressed, class differences mean that the better-off women will gain most. Some women will remain unequal to others unless specific measures to redirect resources and opportunities to women on low incomes are taken.

Specific Measures for Women Who Are Poor

The diagram shows how one group of women in a local centre, the Little Bray Family Resource and Development Centre in County Wicklow, view their poverty. We can see that poverty has many dimensions: emotional, political, financial, social. The 'feelings' element is very strong, as depicted in this diagram, and there are a lot of negative feelings. If we identify the bridges that lead women from poverty, they include:

* education
* adequately paid work
* child care services
* local women's projects
* access to legal services
* good health and health services
* adequate social welfare payments
* proper housing

Women living in poverty lack most if not all of these. Money is a major problem both in terms of inadequate incomes and also because with the cut-backs in public services people now need to buy essential services. Children's schooling, for instance, is no longer free; health services, such as contraception, also cost money.

There are two key elements to women's poverty: dependency and powerlessness.

Dependency

Women's dependence is mainly economic - they are assigned a marginal economic role so they have either no income of their own or their income is inadequate. Social welfare and employment play a major role in keeping women dependent, and they also, of course, are a key to increasing women's independence. The long-term effects of social welfare on women have never been considered - the Commission on Social Welfare, one of the most thorough reviews ever undertaken on the Irish social welfare system, did not make any specific recommendations about the welfare of women working full time in the home.

The tendency to divide women into those who are 'good' and 'deserving' (because their husbands died on them or refused to support them) and those who are 'bad' or 'undeserving' (because they had a child outside of marriage or had too many children) must be avoided. People should be paid on the basis of their need and each individual should get a payment in her or his own right, whatever their marital status. If social welfare payments were paid to each individual, and were adequate, they would help to reduce poverty and women's dependency at the same time. The welfare system should also enable women, and indeed everyone, to be in paid work. As a starting point, people need access to good training and education. Although training and some work schemes exist at present, they do not lead to long-term, well paid work. In any case, most women are excluded from these opportunities because they are not registered as unemployed. Child care responsibilities also exclude women. Affordable training and education opportunities must be made available for women living on low incomes.

Powerlessness

Powerlessness makes you accept your situation as inevitable

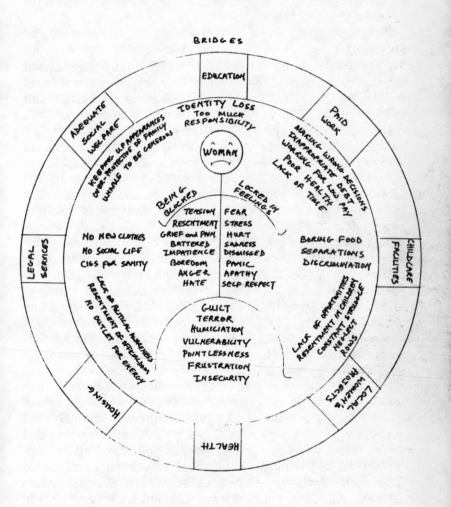

BRIDGES

EDUCATION

PAID WORK

ADEQUATE SOCIAL WELFARE

KEEPING UP APPEARANCES
OVER-PROTECTIVE OF FAMILY
UNABLE TO BE GENEROUS

IDENTITY LOSS
TOO MUCH
RESPONSIBILITY

WOMAN

MAKING WRONG DECISIONS
INAPPROPRIATE DEBT
WORKING FOR LOW PAY
POOR HEALTH
LACK OF TIME

BEING BLOCKED

LOCKED IN FEELINGS

TENSION	FEAR
RESENTMENT	STRESS
GRIEF and PAIN	HURT
BATTERED	SADNESS
IMPATIENCE	DISMISSED
BOREDOM	PANIC
ANGER	APATHY
HATE	SELF RESPECT

NO NEW CLOTHES
NO SOCIAL LIFE
CIGS FOR SANITY

BORING FOOD
SEPARATIONS
DISCRIMINATION

LEGAL SERVICES

CHILDCARE FACILITIES

LACK OF POLITICAL AWARENESS
RESENTMENT OF ATTENDANCE
NO OUTLET FOR ENERGY

GUILT
TERROR
HUMILIATION
VULNERABILITY
POINTLESSNESS
FRUSTRATION
INSECURITY

LACK OF OPPORTUNITIES
RESENTMENT IN CHILDREN
CONSTANT STRUGGLE
NEGLECT
ROWS

HOUSING

LOCAL WOMEN'S PROJECTS

HEALTH

Little Bray Family Resource and Development Centre

125

— its opposite is control. Many women who are poor feel powerless - their lives are controlled from outside - by men, by children or by the state. There are two dimensions to women's powerlessness: in structures and in relationships and attitudes. To increase women's control, specific changes need to occur in each of these domains.

State structures tend to disempower people: it is not easy to get information on services, clear statements of rights are not always available, people have to undergo a complex, often degrading, process to 'prove' that they qualify for a service. Means-testing is very common within social welfare and in other services as well: for books in school, a medical card, welfare payments, rent, and so on. Since women usually interact for the family with the social welfare system, it is they who have to undergo the probing home visits, get the certificates and other forms of proof, often only after a number of trips, and endure the lack of privacy that dependence on social welfare can involve. Some welfare-related procedures can be experienced as deeply degrading. The Supplementary Welfare Allowance (SWA) scheme, for instance, continuously comes up in conversations with women about their poverty. As the discretionary scheme of last resort, SWA is not an entitlement as of right. So, visits to your home may be 'necessary' - to inspect the bed clothes and the hot press to check that replacements really are needed, to ensure that the bed is legless, to look for evidence of a man's presence - if there were, he may be held liable for the up-keep of the woman and her children. Women bear most of the burden of the family's struggle with housing, transport, access to education and other public services and they are often rendered powerless as a result. And yet, people have a right to these services, a right that is not sufficiently asserted or recognised. So, the way applicants and especially women are treated by public services must be changed.

Attitudes and relationships can also disempower women. Men are very powerful and traditional attitudes about women and men remain strong; in many cases women themselves hold traditional attitudes. Education projects are a crucial means of empowering women who are poor, providing not only a social outlet but also new skills. But if change is to be significant, projects must do more than this. First, they must demonstrate to women that they are not alone in their poverty and that their poverty is not their own fault. Secondly, the education process must help to identify the factors that make people poor - to give a sense of perspective on the economic forces that create poverty and show that, while poverty may be outside the control of one individual, it can be challenged by collective action. And the nature of power and how it is exerted must be explored. Projects could lead some way to collective action if they helped women to get in touch with others in a similar situation, within their own area, in other parts of the country and even in other countries. At present, almost one hundred local women's projects exist. They are very popular but most operate on little or no funding. Inadequate funding makes it difficult for projects to undertake the kind of long-term development work that is needed to overcome the effects of poverty. Funding must be made available for democratically-run local educational projects that work to enable their participants to become politically active, at local and national level.

The question of alliances is a difficult one to answer definitively. Women from low income communities have not been significantly involved in the women's movement in Ireland. It is only in the very recent past that women from such communities are themselves mobilising around issues that affect their lives. Activity is fairly piecemeal, however, and tends to have a local rather than a national focus. While this in itself is not a bad thing, a national focus is necessary as well. Women from other classes and men's interest groups or organisations have not generally been involved. It is difficult to know how to proceed. While women from poor communities need to empower themselves and develop their strengths and resources, it will be difficult to achieve change on their own. The struggle is just too big and the opposing forces too strong. So, alliances with other groups and interests will be necessary. But they must be on a selective basis and be informed by a very clear sense of purpose and an acknowledgement that the underlying interests are different.

Challenging men's attitudes and behaviour is crucial. Women's lives are harder because most men fail to take their share of responsibility for the home and children. If women living on low incomes are to challenge the division of labour within the home, they will need the support of their friends and other women. This is another area where collective support for individual action is needed.

However, underlying all of the practices are values and ideologies about women and about men. The same values underlie state structures and practices: the dominance of men and their rightful role as breadwinners. The Constitution itself enshrines women's role as mothers as does the catholic church. The emphasis on the family obscures the welfare of individual family members. All too often, family well-being takes a heavy toll on women. So, unless and until there is a change in ideology, women's situation will remain unchanged.

The women represented in this book are survivors, not victims, exercising immense skill and creative ingenuity in balancing the family's finances and emotions, keeping their families going, working long and hard to shelter their husbands, children and other relatives from the worst excesses of poverty. But a survival existence on or just below the breadline is not a full life. And all women are entitled to that.

FINIS

Heather Brett

It is cold here
at zero level
and the ground is hard
I still hear the thud
as I connected
still remember the wind
rushing in my ears
as I fell
It is lonelier than lonely here
and sometimes I imagine things
sometimes the echo
of my mute cry for help
repeats its ring
and I rise again to all the
repercussions
sometimes my arms ache with phantom
pain
and I remember how I held them up
for so long, empty
and sometimes my eyes are on fire.
There are no tears left.
Nobody broke my fall.

I am getting used to zero level
this place too, has its advantages
never again will I have to beg
for anything
Here, even love can be bought.

CHARTER OF CHANGES NECESSARY TO REDUCE POVERTY AMONG WOMEN

1. Access to an adequate, independent income for all women.

2. Full sharing of family responsibilities and workloads between men and women.

3. Adequate provision for children and all families with children, including state-funded childcare facilities.

4. Adequate and accessible health, education and training, housing, legal and transport services.

5. Adequate funding for local women's projects.

6. Action to deal with unemployment and to create work opportunities that are well paid and that can accommodate workers' family-related responsibilities.

7. Legislative and political changes to improve the economic and social position of women.

FOOTNOTES

INTRODUCTION

1. L. Leghorn and K. Parker, *Women's Worth: Sexual economics and the world of women*. Boston: Routledge and Kegan Paul, 1981, p14.
2. Tim Callan et al, *Poverty and the Social Welfare System in Ireland*. Dublin: Combat Poverty Agency, 1988.
3. Tim Callan et al, *Poverty and the Social Welfare System in Ireland*, p32.
4. Hilda Scott, *Working Your Way to the Bottom*. London: Pandora, 1984, pp19 - 22.
5. See Peter Townsend et al, *Poverty and Labour in London*. London: Low Pay Unit/Poverty Research (London) Trust, 1987, Appendix 2, pp95 - 101 for a good discussion of the measurement of poverty.

CHAPTER 1

6. Beatrix Campbell, *Wigan Pier Revisited: Poverty and politics in the 80s* London: Virago, 1984, p57.
7. Seamus O'Cinneide, 'Poverty and policy: North and South', *Administration*, Vol 33, No 3, 1985.
8. Three research studies are relevant here: Laraine Joyce and Tony McCashin (eds), *Poverty and Social Policy*. Dublin: Institute of Public Administration, 1981; David Rottman et al, *The Distribution of Income in the Republic of Ireland* Dublin: Economic and Social Research Institute, 1982; J. Roche, *Poverty and Income Maintenance Policies in Ireland 1973 - 80* Dublin: Institute of Public Administration, 1984.
9. Tim Callan et al, *Poverty and the Social Welfare System in Ireland*.
10. See, for example, Seamus O'Cinneide, 'The extent of poverty in Ireland', *Social Studies* Vol 1, No 4, August 1972; David Rottman et al, *The Distribution of Income in the Republic of Ireland*. John Roche, *Poverty and Income Maintenance Policies in Ireland, 1973 - 80*.
11. Adjustments have to be made for families of different sizes; these adjustments are known as the equivalence scales. The equivalence scale used most consistently in the initial ESRI report was 1 for the household head, 0.7 for each additional adult and 0.5 for each child. This means for instance that the lowest poverty line for a couple was £54.40 with £16 for each child. At the second cut-off point (£40 for an individual), the poverty line is £68 for a couple plus £20 for each child and at the third poverty line (£48 for one person) it is £81.60 for a couple plus £24 for each child.
12. Hilary Graham, 'Being poor: perceptions and coping strategies of lone mothers', in Julia Brannen and Gail Wilson (eds), *Give and Take in Families: Studies in resource distribution*. London: Allen and Unwin, 1987, p57.
13. We cannot assume that all of these are parenting alone on a long-term basis. Included are women whose husbands or partners were temporarily absent at the time of the Census. So, the figure should be treated with caution.
14. Peter Ward, *The Financial Consequences of Marital Breakdown*. Dublin: Combat Poverty Agency, 1989.
15. Peter Ward, *The Financial Consequences of Marital Breakdown*, p58.
16. Kathleen Newland, *The Sisterhood of Man*. New York: W.W. Norton, 1979.
17. Jane Millar, 'Lone mothers', in Caroline Glendinning and Jane Millar (eds), *Women and Poverty in Great Britain*. Brighton: Wheatsheaf, 1988, pp163 - 4.
18. National Council for the Aged, *Incomes of the Elderly in Ireland*. Dublin: National Council for the Aged, 1984, p106.
19. Sheila Peace, 'The forgotten female: Social policy and older women', in Chris Phillipson and Alan Walker (eds), *Ageing and Social Policy*. Aldershot: Gower, 1986, p75.
20. Joseph Barry and Leslie Daly, *The Travellers' Health Status Study*. Dublin: Health Research Board, 1988. See also David Rottman et al, *The Population Structure and Living*

Circumstances of Irish Travellers: Results from the 1981 census of Traveller families.
Dublin: Economic and Social Research Institute, 1986.

21. Stanislaus Kennedy, *But Where Can I Go?* Dublin: Arlen House, 1985, pp171 - 182.

22. Janice Bell, *Women and Children First.* Dublin: National Campaign for the Homeless, 1989.

23. John Blackwell, *Low Pay and Women.* Dublin: University College, Resource and Environmental Policy Centre, Working Paper No 45, October 1987.

24. Mary Daly and Jim Walsh, *Moneylending and Low Income Families.* Dublin: Combat Poverty Agency, 1988.

25. Eileen Evason, *Just Me and the Kids: A study of single parent families in Northern Ireland.* Belfast: Equal Opportunites Commission, 1980; Hilary Graham, 'Being poor: perceptions and coping strategies of lone mothers', in Julia Brannen and Gail Wilson (eds), *Give and Take in Families,* pp56 -74.

26. Jan Pahl, 'Patterns of money management within marriage', *Journal of Social Policy,* vol 9, no 3, pp313 - 35; Hilary Land, 'Poverty and gender: the distribution of resources within families', in M. Brown (ed), *The Structure of Disadvantage.* London: Heinemann, 1983.

27. Joyce O'Connor at al, *Caring for the Elderly Part 1: A study of carers at home and in the community.* Dublin: Stationery Office, 1988.

CHAPTER 2

28. See Mary Daly (ed), *Women Together Against Poverty.* Dublin: Combat Poverty Agency, KLEAR, DTEDG, 1988.

29. Julia Brannen and Gail Wilson (eds), *Give and Take in Families,* p16.

30. Mary Daly and Jim Walsh, *Moneylending and Low Income Families.*

31. Cited in Sean Stitt, and Monica McWilliams (eds), *A Life of Poverty: Northern Ireland.* Belfast: Social Policy Society and the Northern Ireland Poverty Lobby, 1986, p7.

32. This information comes from case studies carried out for the Combat Poverty Agency and co-ordinated by Patricia Kelleher and Anne Byrne. It is hoped to publish these later in 1989.

33. Hilary Graham, 'Being poor: perceptions and coping strategies of lone mothers' in Julia Brannen and Gail Wilson (eds), *Give and Take in Families,* pp56 - 74.

34. Pauline Lee and Michael Gibney, *Patterns of food and Nutrient Intake in a Suburb of Dublin with chronically high unemployment.* Dublin: Combat Poverty Agency, December, 1988.

35. Mary Daly and Jim Walsh, *Moneylending and Low Income Families.*

36. Mary Daly (ed), *Women Together Against Poverty,* p34.

37. A recent very thorough investigation carried out by the management consultants Craig Gardiner for the Department of Social Welfare found clear evidence of abuse in 1.6% of the unemployment payments and 0.8% of disability benefit payments made in the Dublin area between August 1986 and September 1987.

38. Patricia Kelleher, Adequacy of Social Welfare Payments. Report to the Combat Poverty Agency, 1987.

CHAPTER 3

39. Tony Novak, *Poverty and Social Security* London: Pluto Press, 1984, p61.

40. Irish Times, 3.2.'89.

41. Joyce O'Connor and Mary Lyons, *Enterprise - The Irish approach.* Dublin: Industrial Development Authority, 1983.

42. *Irish Women: Agenda for Practical Action.* Dublin: Stationery Office, 1985, p41.

43. Heather Joshi, 'The cost of caring', in Caroline Glendinning and Jane Millar (eds),

Women and Poverty in Britain, pp112 - 133. 44.

44. Heather Joshi, 'The cost of caring', p114.

45. Margret Fine-Davis, *Changing Gender Role Attitudes in Ireland: 1975 - 1986.* Vol 1. First Report of the Second Joint Committee on Women's Rights, 1988.

46. Margret Fine Davis, *Changing Gender Role Attitudes in Ireland: 1975 - 1986,* Vol 1, p41.

47. Anne McKenna, *Childcare and Equal Opportunities.* Dublin: Employment Equality Agency, 1988, Table 4.5.

48. Margret Fine-Davis, *Changing Gender Role Attitudes in Ireland: 1975 - 1986,* Vol 1, p80.

49. Margret Fine-Davis, *Changing Gender Role Attitudes in Ireland: 1975 - 1986,* Vol 1, p48.

50. John Blackwell, *Women in the Labour Force.* Dublin: Employment Equality Agency, 1989, Table 6.7

51. John Blackwell, *Low Pay and Women,* pp12 - 15. The source for these data is the 1979 Structure of Earnings Survey which examined earnings in industry, wholesale and retail distribution and certain financial services.

52. John Blackwell, *Women in the Labour Force,* 1989.

53. Hilda Scott, *Working Your Way to the Bottom,* pp25 - 28.

54. Hilda Scott, 'Equality Swedish style', *Working Woman,* June, 1982, pp21 - 22.

55. Margret Fine-Davis, *Changing Gender Role Attitudes in Ireland: 1975 - 1986,* Vol 1, pp70 - 71.

56. Margret Fine-Davis, *Changing Gender Role Attitudes in Ireland: 1975 - 1986,* Vol 1, pp70 - 71.

57. John Blackwell, *Women in the Labour Force,* 1986, p5.

58. See Mary Daly, *The Hidden Workers.* Dublin: Employment Equality Agency, 1985, p9.

59. Mary Daly, *The Hidden Workers.*

60. Margret Fine-Davis, *Changing Gender Role Attitudes in Ireland: 1975 - 1986,* Vol 2. Second Report of the Joint Committee on Women's Rights, 1988, pp5 - 15.

61. John Blackwell, *Women in the Labour Force,* 1986, pp63 - 4.

62. Cited in Hilda Scott, *Working Your Way to the Bottom,* p30. See also Ann Oakley, *Housewife.* Harmondsworth: Penguin, p6.

63. James Wickham and Peter Murray, *Women in the Irish Electronics Industry.* Dublin: Employment Equality Agency, 1987.

CHAPTER 4

64. Tony Novak, *Poverty and Social Security,* p54.

65. For information on the different social welfare schemes see Sally Keogh and Ita Mangan, *Social Welfare for Women.* Dublin: Attic Press, 1989.

66. The figures used here exclude women in receipt of maternity benefits/ allowance, smallholder's assistance and supplementary welfare allowance. Conservative estimates have been used where specific figures on the numbers of women claimants were not available. The lack of definite statistics on women's social welfare position reflects official disinterest in how gender affects social welfare patterns.

67. Mary Daly and Jim Walsh, *Moneylending and Low Income Families.*

68. Denis Conniffe and Gary Keogh, *Equivalence Scales and Costs of Children.* Dublin: Economic and Social Research Institute, 1988.

69. Over the last two years the adult dependant's payment has actually fallen as a proportion of that of the main claimant because the Budgets gave a larger increase each time (about 10%) to the main payment than to the adult dependant (about 3%).

70. This is a 'special' or exceptional practice. It is not advertised and, while departmental personnel will assist women who seek help, one must first know about it to seek help.

71. Peter Ward, *The Financial Consequences of Marital Breakdown.* 72. The 1989 Social

Welfare Act introduced some changes in this. First, from 1989 on women will be obliged to hand over any maintenance from their husbands if they wish to receive a deserted wife's payment. Before this, maintenance received from husbands did not generally affect the woman's payment. Secondly, the new legislation also empowered the Minister for Social Welfare to seek maintenance directly from deserting husbands. It does not, however, remove spouses' responsibility to maintain each other so the wife will still have to seek maintenance from her husband, only now she has to hand over whatever amount she gets from him to the state if she wishes to receive a social welfare payment.

73. This does not take account of the fact that rates are also differentiated on the basis of age. The old age pension, for instance, pays different rates to those under and over 80 years and widows, deserted wives and prisoners' wives receive more a week if they are between 66 and 79 years and more again if they are aged 80 or over. This adds another six rates to the ten listed above. Before the changes in the 1989 Budget, there were three more rates: that Budget reduced the number of adult dependant rates for unemployed payments to two (from five).

74. Again, one must add the caution here that some of these low rates are also paid for men. However, there are so few men as dependants in the social welfare system that it is reasonable to assume that the rates for adult dependants reflect the state's evaluation of women rather than men.

75. Joyce O'Connor, et al, *The Caring Process Part 1: A study of carers in the home*.

76. Gillian Pascall, *Social Policy: A feminist analysis*. London: Tavistock, 1988, p198.

77. Jane Millar, 'Lone mothers', in C. Gendinning and J. Millar (eds), *Women and Poverty in Britain*, p174.

CHAPTER 5

78. Hilda Scott, *Working Your Way to the Bottom*, p13.

79. *Adult Education in Disadvantaged Areas: Part One - Adult Literacy*. Department of Education, Discussion Document, 1985, p19.

80. Richard Breen, *Education and the Labour Market: Work and unemployment among recent cohorts of Irish school leavers*. Dublin: Economic and Social Research Institute, 1984, p29.

81. Richard Breen, Education and the Labour Market, p47.

82. Pat Clancy, *Who Goes to College?* Dublin: Higher Education Authority, 1988.

83. David Rottman and Philip O'Connell, 'The changing class structure' in F. Litton (ed), *Unequal Achievement - The Irish experience 1957 - 1982*. Dublin: Institute of Public Administration, 1982, p74.

84. Damian Hannan, Richard Breen et al, *Schooling and Sex Roles: Sex differences in subject provision and student choice in Irish post-primary schools*. Dublin: Economic and Social Research Institute, 1983.

85. Pat Clancy, *Who Goes to College?*.

86. Damian Hannan et al, *Schooling and Sex Roles*.

87. See Pauline Jackson, 'Worlds apart - social dimensions of sex roles' in Pat Clancy et al (eds), *Ireland: A sociological profile*. Dublin: Institute of Public Administration, 1986, pp287 - 306 for a useful discussion.

88. *Women Academics in Ireland*. Dublin: Higher Education Authority, 1987.

89. Madeline MacDonald, 'Schooling and the reproduction of class and gender relations', in Roger Dale et al (eds), *Education and the State* Vol 2. Lewes, Sussex: The Falmer Press, 1981, pp170 - 171.

90. 'Special effects of reduction in expenditure on adult education provision, *AONTAS Newsletter*, Vol 1, No 20, 1988, pp8 - 9.

91. *A Review of Housing Policy*. Dublin: National Economic and Social Council, 1988, pp93 - 117.

92. *A Review of Housing Policy*, pp196 - 199.
93. *A Review of Housing Policy*, p112.
94. *A Review of Housing Policy*, p206.
95. Mary Daly and Jim Walsh, *Moneylending among Low Income Families*, p23. The five local authorities examined were Dublin Corporation, Dublin County Council, Waterford County Borough Council, Cork County Borough Council and Limerick County Council.
96. Patricia Kelleher, *Settling in the City*. Dublin: Focus Point,1988, p93.
97. David Rottman et al, *The Population Structure and Living Circumstances of Irish Travellers: Results from the 1981 census of Traveller families*.
98. *The Population Structure and Living Circumstances of Irish Travellers*, p51.
99. *A Part in Dublin: Accommodation for people out of home: 1986 and 1988*. Dublin: Focus Point, 1988.
100. Peter Ward, *The Financial Consequences of Marital Breakdown*.

CHAPTER 6

101. Gillian Pascall, *Social Policy: A feminist analysis, p165*.
102. Mary Cullen and Terri Morrissey, *Women and Health: Some current issues*. Dublin: Health Education Bureau, 1985, pxv.
103. Mary Daly (ed), *Women Together Against Poverty*.
104. Clare Ungerson (ed), *Women and Social Policy: A reader*. London: Macmillan, 1985, p150.
105. *Positively Healthy: Report from the Council for the Status of Women's Health Conference*. Dublin: Council for the Status of Women, 1988.
106. Mary Daly (ed), *Women Together Against Poverty*, pp40 - 48.
107. *Positively Healthy: Report from the Council for the Status of Women's Health Conference*.
108. See June Levine, *Sisters*. Dublin: Ward River Press, 1982, for a participant's account of the most recent wave of the women's movement in Ireland.
109. Mary Cullen and Terri Morrissey, *Women and Health: Some current issues*, p60.
110. Aileen O'Hare, *'Ireland', The Health Burden of Social Inequities*. Copenhagen: World Health Organization, 1984, p121.
111. Department of Health, *Health Statistics 1987*. Dublin: Stationery Office, 1988, Table G17, p81.
112. *Irish Women: Agenda for practical action*, p136.
113. World Health Organization, *Women and Occupational Health Risks*. Copenhagen: World Health Organization, 1983.
114. Mary Cullen and Terri Morrissey, *Women and Health: Some current issues*, pp35 - 47.
115. Maeve Casey, *Domestic Violence Against Women*. Dublin: Social and Organisational Psychology Research Unit, UCD, nd.
116. Anne Cleary, 'A study of depression among women - implications for preventive mental health'. Paper presented to the International Conference on Mental Health Education, Dublin, September 30, 1986.
117. Mary Cullen and Terri Morrissey, *Women and Health: Some current issues*, pp35 - 47.
118. Gillian Pascall, *Social Policy: A feminist perspective*, p194.
119. Anne Cleary, 'A study of depression among women - implications for preventive mental health'.
120. John Cullen, Tom Ronayne and P. O'Donoghue, Employment, unemployment and the health of women: Impact of own and spouse's employment status'. Research Memo 1, Health Care and Psychosomatic Unit, St James Hospital, Dublin, 1984.
121. See Aileen O'Hare and Aideen O'Connor, 'Gender differences in treated mental illness in the Republic of Ireland', in Chris Curtin et al (eds), *Gender in Irish Society*, p309.
122. Anne Cleary, 'A study of depression among women - implications for preventive mental health', p11.

123. R. Foster, *Health in Rural Ireland: A study of selected aspects.* Dublin and Leitrim: Health Education Bureau and the North Western Health Board, 1984, cited in O'Connor and O'Hare, p321.
124. Aileen O'Hare and Aideen O'Connor, 'Gender differences in treated mental illnesses in the Republic of Ireland', pp314 - 7.
125. Aileen O'Hare and Dermot Walsh, *Activities of Irish Psychiatric Hospitals and Units - 1984.* Dublin: Health Research Board, 1987.
126. *Women's Health Week 11- 19 Oct 1986: Report and Conclusions.* Dublin: Office of Minister of State for Women's Affairs, 1987, pp33 - 42.
127. *Eurobarometer.* Spring 1987, Brussels: European Commission, 1988.
128. M. McSweeney and J. Kevany, *Nutrition Beliefs and Practices in Ireland.* Dublin: Health Education Bureau, 1981.
129. 'Twenty Years of Irish Family Planning', press statement of Irish Family Planning Association, May 19, 1989.
130. Winifred O'Neill, 'A Profile of Family Planning Need', Thesis for Membership (Part Two) of Community Medicine Faculty, Royal College of Physicians, Dublin, October, 1986, unpublished.
131. Antonia Lehane, 'A survey of family planning practices among married women in 10 Irish general practices', *Forum,* Vol 3 No 10, 1987, pp1 - 9.
132. Paul Armstrong and John Rice, 'Family planning and cervical smear patterns in a group of postpartum women', *Forum,* Vol 4, No 6, 1988, pp81 - 86.
133. Aileen O'Hare et al, *Mothers Alone?* Dublin: Federation of Services for Unmarried Parents and their Children, nd, pp24 - 28.
134. Cited in *Irish Women: Agenda for practical action,* pp114 - 5, 327 - 8.
135. Pauline Jackson, 'Outside the jurisdiction: Irish women seeking abortion', in Chris Curtin et al (eds), *Gender in Irish Society,* pp203 - 223.

CHAPTER 7

136. Ursula Barry, 'Women in Ireland - The national question', *Co-options: Women and the Community ,* May 1989, p5.
137. A number of publications give a good outline of the early history of the women's movement in Ireland. See for example, Ailbhe Smyth, 'The contemporary women's movement in the Republic of Ireland', *Women's Studies International Forum,* Vol 11, No 4, 1988, pp331 - 341; Evelyn Mahon, 'Women's rights and Catholicism in Ireland', *New Left Review* 66, 1987, pp53 - 77; Jenny Beale, *Women in Ireland* Dublin: Gill and Macmillan, 1986; Chapter 6; June Levine, *Sisters.* Dublin: Ward River Press, 1982.
138. Ailbhe Smyth, 'The contemporary women's movement in the Republic of Ireland', pp333 - 341.
139. Margret Fine-Davis, *Changing Gender Role Attitudes in Ireland: 1975 - 1976.* Vol 1, pp62 - 67.
140. *The Irish Women's Guidebook and Diary,* produced by Attic Press, contains the most comprehensive listing of women's groups and other relevant organisations.
141. The proceedings of one such meeting have been published: Mary Daly (ed), *Women Together Against Poverty.*
142. *The Register of Completed and Current Work in Women's Studies in Ireland,* compiled by Jean Tansey and Cliona Kernan in 1985, had over 400 entries and at the Interdisciplinary Congress in 1987 up to 100 Irish women presented papers or organised workshops.
143. The list in the current edition of the *Irish Women's Guidebook and Diary* was checked against other sources of information on women's groups, eg applications for funding to the Combat Poverty Agency, the local groups known to the National Social Service Board, AONTAS Adult Education Group members, as well as various local contacts.
144. The six counties with no known women's group are: Cavan, Monaghan, Leitrim, Roscommon, Westmeath, Carlow.

145. Caitriona Nic Giollaphadraigh, *I Am Important: Evaluation of Women's Health and Development Course*. Dublin: Lourdes Youth and Community Services, 1988, p21.

146. See Fran McVeigh, *Women Learning: An account of the women's programmes funded by the Combat Poverty Agency in 1987*. Dublin: Combat Poverty Agency, 1988.

147. Stasia Crickley, 'Women and Community Work: A perspective on the late '80s', *Co-options,* May 1989, pp31 - 33.

CHAPTER 8

148. Tony Novak, *Poverty and Social Security,* pp93 - 94.

149. J. Kincaid, *Poverty and Equality in Britain,* p159.

150. David Rottman et al, *The Distribution of Income in the Republic of Ireland*.

151. Mary Robinson, 'Women and the law in Ireland', *Women's Studies International Forum* Vol 11, No 4, 1988, p351.

152. Irish Transport and General Workers Union, cited in Jenny Beale, *Women in Ireland,* p147.

153. Margret Fine-Davis, *Changing Gender Role Attitudes,* Vol 1, p65.

154. See Finola Kennedy, *Family, Economy and Government in Ireland*. Dublin: Economic and Social Research Institute, 1989, pp64 -65.

155. Peter Ward, *The Financial Consequences of Marital Breakdown*.

156. Delma McDevitt, 'Marriage, maintenance and property' in Chris Curtin, et al (eds), *Gender in Irish Society,* pp224 - 248.

157. Deirdre Curtin, 'Equal treatment in social welfare', in G. Whyte (ed), *Sex Equality, Community Rights and Irish Social Welfare Law*. Dublin: Irish Centre for European Law, 1988, pp16 - 38.

158. See Gerry Whyte, 'Council Directive 79/7/EEC in Ireland', in G. Whyte (ed), *Sex Equality, Community Rights and Irish Social Welfare Law,* pp39 - 59 for a good outline of the main issues in question.

SELECT BIBLIOGRAPHY

BARRY, Ursula, *Lifting the Lid*. Dublin: Attic Press, 1986

BEALE, Jenny, *Women in Ireland* Dublin: Gill & Macmillan, 1986

BLACKWELL, John, *Women in the Labour Force*. Dublin : Employment Equality Agency, 1989

BRANNEN, Jill and Gail WILSON, (eds), *Give and Take in Families: Studies in resource distribution*. London: Allen and Unwin, 1987

BUCKLEY, Mary, and Malcolm ANDERSON, (eds), *Women, Equality and Europe*. London: Macmillan, 1988

BYRNE, Anne, *Women and Poverty: A review of the statistics on low pay, social welfare and the health status of Irish women, 1988*. Dublin: Council for the Status of Women, 1988

CALLAN, Tim, et al, *Poverty and the Social Welfare System in Ireland*. Dublin: Combat Poverty Agency, 1988

CAMPBELL, Beatrix, *Wigan Pier Revisited: Poverty and politics in the 80s*. London: Virago Press, 1984

CLANCY, Pat, et al, (eds), *Ireland: A Sociological Profile*. Dublin: Institute of Public Administration, 1986

Co-Options May 1989

Council for the Status of Women, *Positively Healthy: Report from the Council for the Status of Women's Health Conference*. Dublin: Council for the Status of Women, 1988

CULLEN, Mary and Terri MORRISSEY, *Women's Health: Some current issues*. Dublin: Health Education Bureau, nd

CURTIN, Chris, Pauline JACKSON and Barbara O'CONNOR, (eds), *Gender in Irish Society*. Galway: Galway University Press, 1987

DALY, Mary, *The Hidden Workers*. Dublin: Employment Equality Agency, 1985

DALY, Mary, (ed), *Women Together Against Poverty: The experiences of travelling and settled women in the community*. Dublin: Combat Poverty Agency, KLEAR, DTEDG, 1988

DALY, Mary and Jim WALSH, *Moneylending and Low Income Families*. Dublin: Combat Poverty Agency, 1988

FINE-DAVIS, Margret, *Changing Gender Role Attitudes in Ireland: 1975-1986*. Vols 1,2,3. Report of the Second Joint Committee on Women's Rights, 1988

GLENDINNING, Caroline, and Jane MILLAR, (eds), *Women and Poverty in Britain*. Brighton: Wheatsheaf Books, 1987

HANNAN, Damian and Richard BREEN et al, *Schooling and Sex Roles: Sex differences in subject provision and student choice in Irish post-primary schools*. Dublin: Economic and Social Research Institute, 1983

HARRINGTON, Michael, *The New American Poverty*. London: Firethorne Press, 1984

Irish Women: Agenda for practical action. Dublin: Stationery Office, 1985

Irish Women's Guidebook and Diary, 1989. Dublin: Attic Press, 1988

JENNINGS, Carmel, et al, *Who Owns Ireland - Who Owns You?* Dublin: Attic Press, 1985

KEOGH, Sally and Ita MANGAN, *Social Welfare for Women*. Dublin: Attic Press, 1989

KINCAID, J.C., *Poverty and Inequality in Britain*. Harmondsworth:Penguin, 1973

MCKENNA, Anne, *Childcare and Equal Opportunities*. Dublin: Employment Equality Agency, 1988

MCVEIGH, Fran, *Women Learning: An account of the women's programmes funded by the Combat Poverty Agency in 1987*. Dublin: Combat Poverty Agency, 1988

MAHON, Evelyn, 'Women's rights and Catholicism in Ireland', *New Left Review,* No 166, Nov/Dec 1986, pp53-77

National Economic and Social Council, *Redistribution Through State Social Expenditure in the Republic of Ireland: 1973-1980*. Dublin: National Economic and Social Council, 1988

NOVAK, Tony, *Poverty and Social Security*. London: Pluto Press, 1984

PASCALL, Gillian, *Social Policy: A feminist analysis*. London: Tavistock, 1986

Report of the Commission on Social Welfare. Dublin: Stationery Office, 1986

SCOTT, Hilda, *Working Your Way to the Bottom: The Feminization of Poverty*. London: Pandora Press, 1984

SMYTH, Ailbhe, (ed), 'Feminism in Ireland' *Women's Studies International Forum,* Vol 11, No 4. Dublin: Attic Press/New York: Pergamon, 1988

TANSEY, Jean, *Women in Ireland: A compilation of relevant data*. Dublin: Council for the Status of Women, 1984

WARD, Peter, *The Financial Consequences of Marital Breakdown*. Dublin: Combat Poverty Agency, 1989

INDEX

LIFTING THE LID
Handbook of Facts and Information on Ireland
Ursula Barry

'Ursula Barry's digest of facts and information presents the low down on Ireland in an accessible and highly readable form. *Lifting the Lid* makes it clear why the fight for women's demands will be at the centre of any future challenge to the entrenched interests of church, state and capital in Ireland.' *City Limits*

SOCIAL WELFARE FOR WOMEN

This handbook, *Social Welfare for Women* is much needed and long overdue. It will be welcomed by all women who depend on Social Welfare for survival. Despite the complexities of the system, *Social Welfare for Women* succeeds in presenting the facts clearly and concisely.

If you want to know your rights and entitlements as a single parent, as a carer of children or of the elderly, as a young unemployed adult, as a widow or a member of a religious order then this is definitely the book for you.

Sally Keogh is an Information Officer with the National Social Services Board, and has been a regular contributor to the 'Gay Byrne Radio Hour' answering queries on entitlement issues. *Ita Mangan* is the author of *Entitlements for the Elderly, Entitlements for the Disabled* and *Entitlements for the Unemployed*.

112pp ISBN: 0946211 604 £2.95

For further information and a copy of our catalogue, please send a stamped addressed envelope to:
Attic Press
44 East Essex Street
Dublin 2 Ireland

FEMINISM IN IRELAND
Women's Studies International Forum - Special Issue
Ailbhe Smyth (Guest Editor)

A selection of the most stimulating contributions from the Women's Worlds Festival and Congress held in Dublin, July 1987.

Attic Press has purchased a limited number of copies of this special edition on 'Feminism in Ireland' which will be available by mail-order only from **Attic Press**, at £9.95

This is a unique collection of writing by women active in a wide range of spheres, reflecting the diverse responses of Irish women to the issues and experiences confronting them today. The socio-political realities and the cultural and creative needs of women in Ireland are explored by community and movement activists, by academics and by creative writers and artists.

The relationship between feminism and the state is analysed from a variety of perspectives, both historical and contemporary, including significant assessments of the development and impact of the women's movement, the effects of partition and British Imperialism, the role of the Catholic Church in the construction of ideology. Poverty, emigration, lesbianism, divorce and the legal system, are only some of the urgent, often controversial issues brought into focus in this collection. Contributors include: Eavan Boland, Anne O'Connor, Angela Bourke, Jo Murphy-Lawless, Ros Cowman, Bairbre de Brún, Rita Kelly, Mary Robinson, Noreen Byrne, Anne Le Marquand Hartigan, Joni Crone, Cathleen O'Neill, Bríona Nic Dhiarmada, Nuala Ní Dhómhnaill, Pauline Cummins, Ursula Barry, Evelyn Conlon etc.